WISDOM IN PROVERBS

STUDIES IN BIBLICAL THEOLOGY

WISDOM IN PROVERBS

The Concept of Wisdom in Proverbs 1–9

R. N. WHYBRAY

WIPF & STOCK · Eugene, Oregon

Wipf and Stock Publishers
199 W 8th Ave, Suite 3
Eugene, OR 97401

Wisdom in Proverbs
By Whybray, R. N.
Copyright©1965 SCM Press
ISBN 13: 978-1-60899-019-1
Publication date 9/15/2009
Previously published by SCM Press, 1965

Copyright © SCM Press 1965
First English edition 1965 by SCM Press
This Edition published by arrangement with SCM-Canterbury Press

CONTENTS

	Preface	7
	Abbreviations	9
I	PROVERBS 1–9 AND THE PROBLEM OF WISDOM	11
II	THE BOOK OF THE TEN DISCOURSES	33
	THE TEN DISCOURSES	37
III	THE TEN DISCOURSES AND THE EGYPTIAN INSTRUCTIONS: FUNDAMENTAL CONCEPTS	53
	A. THE EGYPTIAN INSTRUCTIONS	53
	1. The concept of *maat*	54
	2. The gods	56
	3. The ideal man	59
	4. The nature of authority and the purpose of the instructions	61
	B. THE TEN DISCOURSES	61
	1. The concept of Order	61
	2. Doctrine of God	63
	3. The ideal man	65
	4. The nature of authority and the purpose of the discourses	67
	C. CONCLUSIONS	69
IV	THE DEVELOPMENT OF THE CONCEPT OF WISDOM	72
	A. TWO TYPES OF WISDOM PASSAGE	72
	B. THE FIGURE OF WISDOM: FIRST STAGE	76
	1. The personification theory	80
	2. The mythological theories	82
	3. A Canaanite goddess of wisdom?	83
	4. Supposed mythological features	87
	5. The purpose and function of the wisdom passages	92
	C. THE FIGURE OF WISDOM: SECOND STAGE	95
	1. The 'fear' of Yahweh	95
	2. The divine origin of wisdom	98

Contents

V	Epilogue	105
	Select Bibliography	108
	Index of Authors	111
	Index of References	113
	Index of Subjects	118

PREFACE

As the subtitle indicates, this book is a study of a small section of the Book of Proverbs: chapters 1–9. No attempt has been made to examine the book as a whole or to trace the further development of the concept of wisdom in the literature of later Judaism. Nevertheless it will, I hope, be clear from the argument that these chapters, properly understood, illuminate the study of the wider problems of wisdom in Israel. The reasons for this conclusion are stated in the latter part of the first chapter and in the Epilogue.

The main thesis of the book is that these chapters are not a literary unity expressing a single concept of wisdom, but consist of an original lesson-book designed for use in scribal schools and closely modelled on Egyptian prototypes, to which later writers have added interpretative material with the intention of bringing its teaching more closely into conformity with Israelite religious beliefs: it is in this additional material that wisdom appears, having been developed as a means to this end. Various views concerning the origin of this figure of wisdom are discussed, and the conclusion is reached that although in some passages it has been depicted in language borrowed from foreign mythology, it is and remains essentially an attribute of Yahweh. Its personification here, however, provided a starting-point for the bolder hypostatization of wisdom which we find in Ecclesiasticus and the Wisdom of Solomon.

This study has been prefaced by an introductory chapter, in conformity with the general purposes of this series, mainly devoted to a brief sketch of the problems of the history of wisdom in Israel and a survey of the present state of knowledge. It is intended mainly for those readers who may not be familiar with the subject.

Exigencies of space have made it necessary to curtail somewhat drastically the detailed discussion of the views of earlier writers on the text and interpretation of these chapters, and the detailed comparison of the original lesson-book with foreign wisdom literature which were included when the book was originally

Preface

submitted as a doctoral thesis to the University of Oxford. These works have, however, been carefully studied and weighed, and I hope to publish more detailed discussions of some points later in the form of articles.

Since the completion of the book in its original form at least two new commentaries on Proverbs (those of Schneider and Ringgren) have been published, and a second edition of Gemser's commentary has appeared. Although no reference is made to them in this book, I have consulted them; but I have found nothing there which necessitates any modification of my arguments or conclusions.

Finally, in addition to a grateful acknowledgment of my debt to earlier scholarship, I wish to record my deep appreciation of the generous assistance given to me by Professor G. R. Driver of Magdalen College, Oxford, both for his criticisms and suggestions and for drawing my attention to many relevant articles which otherwise I should have missed; to Professor H. H. Rowley, who also kindly supplied me with bibliographical material; and, among those who have read the typescript at various stages, to Professor Peter Ackroyd, who first suggested publication, and to Professor James Barr of Princeton. I am also most grateful to the Kennicott Trustees at Oxford for the Fellowship which made it possible for this study to be undertaken, and especially to the Dean of Christ Church, Dr C. A. Simpson, for many kindnesses.

R. N. WHYBRAY

Karuizawa, Japan
July 1964

ABBREVIATIONS

AJSL	*American Journal of Semitic Languages and Literatures*
ANET	*Ancient Near Eastern Texts Relating to the Old Testament,* ed. by J. B. Pritchard, Princeton, 1950; 2nd ed., 1955
ATD	Das Alte Testament Deutsch, ed. by V. Herntrich and A. Weiser, Göttingen
BASOR	*Bulletin of the American Schools of Oriental Research*
BH	*Biblia Hebraica,* ed. by R. Kittel, text edited by P. Kahle, A. Alt and O. Eissfeldt, Stuttgart, 1951
BOT	De Boeken van het Oude Testament, ed. by W. Grossouw *et al.,* Roermond
BSOAS	*Bulletin of the School of Oriental and African Studies*
BZAW	Beihefte zur *Zeitschrift für die alttestamentliche Wissenschaft*
Erman	A. Erman, *The Literature of the Ancient Egyptians* (tr. by A. M. Blackman), London, 1927
G.-K.	*Gesenius' Hebrew Grammar,* edited and enlarged by E. Kautzsch, 2nd English edition revised by A. E. Cowley, Oxford, 1910
HAT	Handbuch zum Alten Testament, ed. by O. Eissfeldt, Tübingen
ICC	The International Critical Commentary, ed. by S. R. Driver, A. Plummer and C. A. Briggs, Edinburgh
JBL	*Journal of Biblical Literature*
JEA	*Journal of Egyptian Archaeology*
JTS	*Journal of Theological Studies*

Abbreviations

KHAT	Kurzer Hand-Commentar zum Alten Testament, ed. by K. Marti, Freiburg i. B.
LXX	The Septuagint Version of the Old Testament
MT	The Massoretic Text of the Old Testament
NTT	*Nieuw Theologisch Tijdschrift*
RB	*Revue Biblique*
RES	*Revue des Etudes Sémitiques*
RGG²	*Die Religion in Geschichte und Gegenwart*, 2nd ed., Tübingen
RHPR	*Revue d'Histoire et de Philosophie religieuses*
SB	La Sainte Bible, ed. by L. Pirot and A. Clamer, Paris
SBJ	*La Sainte Bible traduite en français sous la direction de l'Ecole Biblique de Jérusalem*, Paris
SHAW	*Sitzungsberichte der Heidelberger Akademie der Wissenschaften, Phil.-hist. Klasse*
SPAW	*Sitzungsberichte der Preussischen Akademie der Wissenschaften, Phil.-hist. Klasse*
TLZ	*Theologische Literaturzeitung*
VT	*Vetus Testamentum*
VT Suppl.	Supplements to *Vetus Testamentum*
ZAW	*Zeitschrift für die alttestamentliche Wissenschaft*
ZDMG	*Zeitschrift der Deutschen Morgenländischen Gesellschaft*

I

PROVERBS 1-9 AND THE PROBLEM OF WISDOM

IN attempting to give a more systematic formulation to their beliefs than had previously been achieved, the theological writers of later Judaism found a unifying principle in the concept of the wisdom of God, of which it has been said that it 'increasingly became the form *par excellence* in which all Israel's later theological thought moved', and that 'the entire theological thinking of later Judaism came more or less under the sway of wisdom: at any rate it found in the general concept a unity and an all-embracing factor such as Israel had not possessed until then'.[1]

This wisdom (Heb. *ḥokmā*, occasionally *ḥokmōt*; Gk σοφία), which is associated in the later literature with the word of God, the Spirit of God, and the Law, is represented in Ecclesiasticus and the Wisdom of Solomon[2] as something more than an impersonal divine attribute. It is a distinct hypostasis or divine being, created by and dependent on God but possessing an existence of its own: an associate of God in his divine work of the creation and maintenance of the world, and sent by him to dwell among men, and especially in Israel, to guide and instruct them and to confer God's gifts on them.

This concept was a factor of some importance in the development of the theology of the Early Church. The New Testament doctrine of Christ especially bears the marks of its influence. St Paul declares that Christ is himself the incarnate wisdom of God (I Cor. 1.24; cf. Col. 2.3); the Christological formula in Col. 1.15–17 shows the influence of Wisd. 7; and wisdom is one of the concepts underlying the Logos in St John's Gospel.

The identification of wisdom with Christ was pursued in the

[1] G. von Rad, *Old Testament Theology* I, Edinburgh and London, 1962, p. 441.
[2] Esp. Ecclus 1; 24; Wisd. 7ff.

Wisdom in Proverbs

patristic period, particularly in the writings of the Greek Fathers, and in exegesis the figure of wisdom in Proverbs, Ecclesiasticus and Wisdom was interpreted Christologically. Outside orthodox circles, wisdom held a peculiar attraction for curious minds, and played an important part in Gnostic speculation as a divine emanation through which both the creation and the redemption of the world were accomplished.

In the Old Testament, while the idea of wisdom both as a human attribute and as a gift of God appears frequently, especially in the books of Proverbs, Job and Ecclesiastes, it is represented in the form of a person only in a few passages, all of which occur in Prov. 1–9.[1] Since these are the earliest examples of the personification of wisdom in Jewish literature, and—especially Prov. 8.22–31—the principal source of the later personifications in Ecclesiasticus and Wisdom which in turn influenced the New Testament writers, they are of crucial importance for the understanding of the later developments in Judaism and Christianity. It is the purpose of the present study to re-examine the origin and purpose of this figure of wisdom.

It has always been something of an enigma, and has been interpreted in a variety of ways. The three passages primarily concerned are 1.20–33; 8.1–35; 9.1–6. In the first two of these wisdom is represented as a woman who stands in the public places of the city and appeals to men to receive her instruction. In two long speeches she asserts that those who do so will find that it brings them every kind of happiness and prosperity. In the course of the speech in ch. 8 she makes even greater claims: it is she who gives to the rulers of the nations of the world their authority and ability to rule (8.15f.). Here wisdom reveals her identity, for these are gifts which belong to God alone. This is no mere human wisdom but the wisdom of God himself. This is made even clearer in 8.22–31, where she gives an account of her origins, saying that she is the first of God's creatures, created before the beginning of the world and a witness of all his creative acts. In 9.1–6 wisdom appears again as a woman who invites

---

[1] In a few other passages—e.g. Job 28—wisdom is objectified as an infinitely precious commodity. Such objectification may be a first step towards personification (see ch. IV, *infra*), but does not present the same kind of theological problem.

passers-by to a feast at her house which will confer on them life and understanding, in contrast to the attractions offered by 'the woman Folly' (9.13–18) who invites them to a feast of pleasure which ends in death.

There are other examples in the Old Testament of extended and elaborate personifications, where it is clear that the figures are allegorical and not to be regarded as real persons;[1] but in the case of these passages which represent wisdom as a person there are circumstances which have given rise to the view that something more than a mere literary metaphor is intended: that in the mind of the author wisdom had assumed a degree of reality as a being distinguishable from, though not independent of, God, a divine agent rather than merely a divine characteristic. There are three main reasons for this view: firstly the fact that the figure of wisdom was unquestionably so regarded in later literature which is partly dependent on these passages; secondly that there are instances of similar phenomena in the development of 'hypostases' from divine attributes in other near-eastern religions with which the Israelite author will have been familiar; and thirdly that certain features in the description of wisdom here suggest that foreign mythological influence was at work.

The question of the nature of this personification cannot be separated from the question of its purpose; and this in turn must be discussed in relation to the context of the passages concerned: that is, to Prov. 1–9 as a whole; for it is clear from their contents that they are not isolated fragments which have found their way into Prov. 1–9 by chance, but that their theme is closely related to the teaching of the other chapters. The divine wisdom which is personified in these few passages speaks in language which at some points closely resembles that which is used elsewhere about the wisdom of a human teacher, and her representation as a woman, especially in 9.1–6, where she is said to invite men to a feast at her house, contains features which are evidently intended to echo not merely the counter-invitation of the woman Folly in 9.13–18 but also that of another figure, the 'strange' or adulterous woman of 3.16ff.; 7.5–27, etc. In view of this clear relationship

[1] E.g. the allegory of the two unchaste sisters who stand for Samaria and Jerusalem in Ezek. 23. Here although the author may have used mythological or legendary sources the use which he makes of them is metaphorical.

with the rest of Prov. 1–9, which consists mainly of instruction given by a teacher to his pupil, it has been argued that the purpose of the personification is nothing more than an attempt by the teacher to give a lively character to his teaching by presenting it in personal terms. Other scholars, on the other hand, have found this explanation insufficient, and have pointed out a number of features which seem to indicate the influence of mythological themes. But in either case the questions of the origin and of the purpose of the figure of wisdom cannot properly be discussed apart from a study of Prov. 1–9 as a whole.

This in turn necessitates placing Prov. 1–9 in its setting as a product of a distinct tradition in the life and thought of ancient Israel—the wisdom tradition. We therefore begin this study with a short sketch of the wisdom tradition in Israel, as far as the evidence permits us to do so.

The wisdom literature of the Old Testament[1] is clearly distinguishable both in form and contents from the other main types of Old Testament literature such as history, law, prophecy and psalms. It occupies, indeed, an entirely unique position, for whereas the other types are all firmly rooted in the specific religious tradition of Israel and are concerned exclusively with its life and institutions, the wisdom books say nothing whatever about Israel, its history and political vicissitudes, its peculiar status as the people of God, its cult, laws, priesthood or prophets. In these books the centre of interest is the individual with his needs, ambitions and problems; and even when the problems of the relation of the individual to society are discussed it is human society in general rather than the specific community of Israel to which reference is made.

Thus one might conclude from reading these books that their authors were men who took no interest in the political or religious life of Israel. This, however, would be a serious mistake. What these books show us is that there were more sides to Israelite life and thought than the other books of the Old Testament permit us to see. The Israelite was no less a many-sided man than his contemporaries. Like them, he used his reasoning powers in an

[1] Proverbs, Job and Ecclesiastes. A few Psalms and occasional passages in other books should also be classed as wisdom literature.

attempt to understand the world around him. His reasoning was not in principle opposed to his faith, but it was used, at first at least, in relation to aspects of life concerning which his specifically religious teaching gave him no information or guidance. The knowledge thus acquired, which the Israelite called 'wisdom', was essentially practical: the attempt to understand the nature of things was dictated not so much by intellectual curiosity as by man's practical need to control his environment sufficiently to be able to survive and flourish; and 'wisdom' covered a wide range of such useful information, from skill in using tools to a knowledge of the art of personal relationships. It also included the skilful use of language, such as is displayed in the making of proverbs, riddles, etc.[1]

The wisdom books of the Old Testament may be said, in a sense, to be products of this process of practical reasoning in Israel; but they are not the products of the Israelite genius entirely unaided. It is hardly surprising that they show signs of foreign influence. Israel at no time lived a life of isolation, and was, especially in its early days, inevitably the pupil of the superior, ancient civilizations of Egypt and Mesopotamia. The books of Proverbs, Job and Ecclesiastes probably contain some examples of 'native' popular wisdom of the kind found occasionally in the historical books of the Old Testament,[2] but on the whole they belong to a specifically *literary* wisdom tradition which, though no doubt it took its origin from a pre-literary, relatively unsophisticated reflection on the nature of human life, had been sophisticated and practised as a literary art by the educated classes in Egypt and Mesopotamia for something like two millennia before Israel came into existence. Within this tradition there were more than one type of literary composition. Of the extant examples, some are wholly didactic, others reflective or meditative. A comparison of the Old Testament wisdom books with this foreign literature has shown that the relation of the former to the latter is not merely one of parallel development within a common tradition, but rather of the adoption by Israelites of a specific literary tradition which, at least in some respects, they copied closely. This is perhaps particularly true in the case of Proverbs. Forty years ago A. Erman

[1] For a full discussion of this subject see von Rad, *op. cit.*, pp. 418–29.
[2] E.g. Judg. 9.8, 15; 14.14, 18; II Kings 14.9.

demonstrated conclusively the existence of a direct literary relationship between the Egyptian *Instruction of Amen-em-opet*[1] and Prov. 22.17–23.11.[2] It is possible that the discovery of other examples of Egyptian didactic literature may reveal further proof of literary borrowing; but even without such additional evidence the strong resemblance of the Old Testament wisdom books to non-Israelite wisdom literature of an earlier period in many respects (subject, setting, style, language) is sufficient to show that the Israelite authors, however much they may have adapted and modified it, must be regarded as borrowers of a foreign literary tradition.

In the case of the didactic type of wisdom literature of which Proverbs is an example, our knowledge of the foreign—especially Egyptian—works known as 'instructions' and their background, which is relatively complete, enables us to place Proverbs in its proper setting in the life of Israel despite the almost complete silence of the Old Testament on that subject. The purpose of the Egyptian instructions was the education of the young, and the place where they were used was the classroom.

The Egyptians (and also the Babylonians, although our information about the latter is less complete) maintained from very early times schools in which young pupils from the upper class were trained to be scribes, that is, equipped to occupy the leading positions in the government of the country. To be a scribe was to belong to the privileged, relatively leisured and cultured class—an advantage which, though obvious to his elders, the young pupil did not always appreciate, and of which he had to be convinced, as many of the educational texts show.[3] The knowledge and skill required to be a scribe was something to which no one else had access, and so the teacher himself was a scribe, whose task was

---

[1] Translation in F. Ll. Griffith, 'The Teaching of Amenophis, the son of Kanekht', *JEA* 12, 1926, pp. 191–231. Quotations in the following pages are taken from this translation. A new translation of most of *Amen-em-opet* is given in *ANET*, pp. 421–4, with a select bibliography on the subject.

[2] A. Erman, 'Eine ägyptische Quelle der "Sprüche Salomos"', *SPAW*, 1924, pp. 86–93. Sporadic attempts to prove that the Egyptian work is dependent on a Hebrew source, of which the most recent is that of E. Drioton, 'Sur la Sagesse d'Aménopé' in *Mélanges Bibliques rédigés en l'honneur d'André Robert*, Paris, 1957, pp. 254–80, have not met with general acceptance.

[3] For a detailed study of Egyptian education, see H. Brunner, *Altägyptische Erziehung*, Wiesbaden, 1957.

Proverbs 1–9 and the Problem of Wisdom

to hand down this special craft to the next generation, as in more ancient times it had been handed down from father to son. Since the basis of the teaching was the ability to read and write, the scribal class (which included the priests) and the cultured class were virtually the same. So it is probable that the meditative or quasi-philosophical works of Egyptian literature, though probably not primarily didactic in intention, were also produced by the same class. This was probably the case also in Israel, whose wisdom literature includes both the didactic Proverbs and Ecclesiasticus and the more reflective Job and Ecclesiastes.[1]

Teaching in the Egyptian wisdom schools was severely practical. In addition to reading, writing and other rudiments the pupil was taught the rules for success and happiness in life which were the product of the experience of many generations. No distinction was made between the prudential and the ethical, the religious and the secular, the social good and the individual good. Human life was seen as a whole, and in every situation there was a right and a wrong way of behaving, which led respectively to happiness and disaster, to life and to death.

There is little doubt about the means through which Israel derived its knowledge of this foreign tradition of literary wisdom. During the monarchy there was, as the books of Kings, Isaiah and Jeremiah show, a class of officials at court known as 'scribes' (*sōpᵉrîm*) whose functions were, broadly speaking, the same as those of the scribes of Egypt, Mesopotamia and other countries. There is some reason to suppose that these, like their foreign counterparts, formed an intellectual *élite*.[2] It is also certain that they had international contacts. Some of them, as government officials, were responsible for international correspondence and diplomacy,[3]

---

[1] The term 'wisdom literature' is, strictly speaking, only applicable to the Israelite books, since in the foreign literature the word 'wisdom' is not used in the same way as a technical term. In fact, however, it is commonly used to cover both Israelite and foreign literature of this type, and this practice has been followed here.

[2] In Israel they were not, however, the only educated class, since at least from the time of Isaiah writing was used by such people as prophets (Isa. 8.1), and there is an extensive priestly literature (priests and scribes being separate groups in Israel) some of which was almost certainly committed to writing early. If Judg. 8.14 refers to writing, literacy may have been fairly common in Palestine from an early date.

[3] Note, e.g., the part played by Shebna the scribe in the diplomatic negotiations with the Assyrian ambassador in Isa. 36, and his request that they be

and were in touch with their opposite numbers abroad. Indeed, some of them may actually have been foreigners in the employ of the kings of Israel.[1] Much of the organization and ceremonial of the early monarchy was borrowed from abroad.[2] It was natural that the demands suddenly made upon native Israelite administrative resources by the lightning growth of political power in the reign of David should have had to be supplied from the resources of friendly foreign powers. The Egyptian idea of the superiority of the scribal profession over all others, which appears so often in Egyptian literature, still left its imprint on Jewish scribes as late as the time of Ecclesiasticus, where this theme is treated in a manner remarkably similar to its treatment in Egypt a millennium and a half earlier.[3]

The probability that it was through the scribes, with their international connexions, that foreign wisdom was introduced into Israel is strengthened by the close relationship between the words 'wise man' (*ḥākām*) and 'scribe' (*sōpēr*). 'Wise men' was a term used for teachers of wisdom, and two of the collections in Proverbs are specifically attributed to them (Prov. 22.17; 24.23). But in Jer. 18.18 the term is used, apparently in a technical sense, to designate a specific class of men who, together with the priests and the prophets, constituted the basis of established society at that time. Each of these groups is here said to have its distinctive function. The priests possess the *tōrā*, the prophets the 'word', and the wise men 'counsel' (*'ēṣā*). Both the context of this verse and the meaning of *'ēṣā* elsewhere[4] show that the function here ascribed to the wise men is that of adviser to the king. Thus in Israel the wise men, among whom were numbered the authors of wisdom books, occupied those high offices of state which in Israel, as in other countries, are elsewhere said to have been

---

carried on in Aramaic, the language of diplomacy which was not understood by the ordinary inhabitants of Jerusalem.

[1] On the evidence for this see R. de Vaux, 'Titres et fonctionnaires égyptiens à la cour de David et de Salomon', *RB* 48, 1939, pp. 394-405; J. Begrich, 'Sōfēr und Mazkīr', *ZAW* 58, 1940, pp. 1-29.
[2] See the bibliography on this subject in R. de Vaux, *Ancient Israel: Its Life and Institutions*, Oxford, 1961, pp. 526-8.
[3] Ecclus 38.24ff. Cf. Erman, pp. 189-98; *ANET*, pp. 432-4.
[4] See P. A. H. De Boer, 'The Counsellor', *Wisdom in Israel* (VT Suppl. 3), Leiden, 1955, pp. 42-71.

Proverbs 1–9 and the Problem of Wisdom

occupied by scribes.[1] While we cannot know whether the two classes were exactly identical, it is clear that scribes and wise men were at least very closely associated.

We may therefore conclude that the main reason for the borrowing of the foreign wisdom tradition was educational. As in Egypt, so in Israel the wisdom books were at first used in the training of young men to become scribes. There is, it is true, no mention of scribal schools in the Old Testament (unless the house built by Wisdom in Prov. 9.1 is a school); but it is generally recognized that the relatively highly organized Israelite state of monarchical times presupposes a more thorough system of education for its political leaders and administrative officers than can have been provided by the personal instruction of children by their own parents.[2] Such scribal schools may at first have been mainly foreign in character: this is suggested by the fact that Prov. 22.17–23.11 at least is based on an Egyptian original. But even this is by no means a mere translation. The Israelite wisdom teachers began, probably quite early, to adapt their Egyptian models in accordance with local requirements; and the collections in Proverbs show that they eventually composed their own instructions, still keeping, however, in general to the foreign tradition which they had made their own.

The lack of reliable specific indications makes it difficult to know exactly when foreign wisdom was first introduced into Israel. The general consensus of older scholarship was that wisdom only appeared in Israel at a comparatively late date; but more recently there has been an increasing tendency to allow that some parts of Proverbs may be pre-exilic.[3] Unfortunately the only

---

[1] E.g. Seraiah, II Sam. 8.17; Sheva, II Sam. 20.25; Shebna, II Kings 18.18; Shaphan, II Kings 22.8.

[2] A. Klostermann, 'Schulwesen im alten Israel', *Theologische Studien Theodor Zahn . . . dargebracht*, Leipzig, 1908, pp. 193–232; L. Dürr, *Das Erziehungswesen im Alten Testament und im Antiken Orient*, Leipzig, 1932, pp. 107–12; A. Bentzen, *Introduction to the Old Testament* I, Copenhagen and London, 1948, pp. 171f.

[3] This is the result partly of the discovery in Egyptian and Mesopotamian works of undoubted antiquity of ideas which had previously been thought to have first appeared in Greek thought; partly of the realization, based on such evidence as wisdom texts in the Amarna Letters, that there was an ancient wisdom tradition in Canaan before the arrival of the Israelites. However, attempts such as that of W. F. Albright ('Some Canaanite-Phoenician sources of Hebrew wisdom', *Wisdom in Israel* [VT Suppl. 3], 1955, pp. 1–15) to show

demonstrable literary connexion—with *Amen-em-opet*—is of no use in this matter, as the date of *Amen-em-opet* is also uncertain. The ascription of the whole of Proverbs to Solomon (1.1) is not to be taken seriously, but it is difficult to set aside entirely the persistent tradition which connects Solomon with wisdom. Apart from the tradition about Solomon's wisdom in I Kings, two of the collections in Proverbs are assigned to Solomon.[1] The argument for assigning some parts of the book to the pre-exilic period is supported by those passages which speak of the character of kings and the right way to approach them[2] and by the mention of the activity of the 'men of Hezekiah' in 25.1, a section which begins with a series of proverbs about kings.[3]

The ascription of wisdom to Solomon may have a historical basis in the sense that, whether he himself was or was not wise in any of the senses in which the author of I Kings ascribes wisdom to him, his may have been the reign in which foreign wisdom was introduced with royal encouragement. The political and cultural conditions were then extremely favourable for this. Politically Solomon was strongly orientated towards Egypt, and also maintained close relations with other countries which possessed a wisdom tradition;[4] while his reign has been described as one of great cultural advance.[5] Thus the traditions which represent him as playing a leading part in the international wisdom discourse of

---

that Canaanite wisdom exercised great influence on Israelite wisdom are bound to fall short of proof, in the total absence of a corpus of Canaanite wisdom literature. See further pp. 83ff., *infra*.

[1] 10.1ff.; 25.1ff.
[2] 14.28, 35; 16.10–15; 19.12; 20.2, 8, 26, 28; 21.1; 22.11, 29; 24.21; 25.2–7; 29.4, 14.
[3] For a recent study of the collections in Prov. 10–29 see U. Skladny, *Die ältesten Spruchsammlungen in Israel*, Göttingen, 1962.
[4] For the wisdom of Tyre see Ezek. 28. There is probably a historical basis to the story of the visit of the Queen of Sheba (I Kings 10.1–13), though the statement about Solomon's superiority to foreign wisdom in I Kings 4.29–34 (Heb. 5.9–14) probably comes from a later time. On Solomon's wisdom see A. Alt, 'Die Weisheit Salomos', *TLZ* 76, 1951, pp. 139–44 = *Kleine Schriften zur Geschichte des Volkes Israel* II, Munich, 1959, pp. 90–99; cf. B. Gemser, *Sprüche Salomos* (HAT), 1937, p. 2. R. B. Y. Scott, 'Solomon and the Beginnings of Wisdom in Israel', *Wisdom in Israel* (VT Suppl. 3), pp. 262–79, questions the evidence concerning Solomon and suggests the reign of Hezekiah as the time of the introduction of foreign wisdom into Israel.
[5] K. Galling, *Die Krise der Aufklärung in Israel*, Mainz, 1951.

his time, and the ascription of certain collections in Proverbs to him may not be entirely unfounded. It is not unreasonable to suppose that his court, like other royal courts of the time, was the scene of cultural activity, with his scribes forming an intellectual *élite* and with a scribal school ensuring that the tradition was handed down to the next generation.

The subsequent history and development of wisdom in Israel, however, still unfortunately remain largely obscure. In Ecclesiasticus, written in the second century, we see what it eventually became—a handmaid of orthodox Judaism. Wisdom has become identified with the Law; and the scribe or wise man—the two are identical—is one who, while he possesses other knowledge as well, makes the Law the principal object of his study. Wisdom has become 'nationalized' or 'judaized'. It has also become fully hypostatized. But the Old Testament gives us almost no direct information about when or how these changes took place during the eight centuries which separate Ben Sira from Solomon. Outside the wisdom literature itself, direct references to wisdom and the wise men in the Old Testament are few: some examples of popular proverbs, riddles, etc., in the historical books, some allusions to professional 'wise women' in the early monarchy,[1] a few comments in the pre-exilic prophets, some references to the wise men of Egypt in Genesis and Exodus, and the traditions of Solomon's wisdom in I Kings, some of which may reflect a later concept of wisdom. In addition, recent study has revealed the presence of the influence of wisdom in the prophetical books,[2] and the story of Joseph in Genesis has been interpreted as designed to present the hero as an ideal figure who embodies all the virtues taught in the wisdom schools.[3]

Of these references it is only the comments of Isaiah and Jeremiah on the wise men and their wisdom which throw any direct light on the way in which wisdom was regarded by people outside the wisdom circles at any time during this period. In these prophetic judgments we see the mutual confrontation of two

[1] II Sam. 14.2; 20.16.
[2] J. Lindblom, 'Wisdom in the Old Testament Prophets', *Wisdom in Israel* (VT Suppl. 3), pp. 192–204.
[3] G. von Rad, 'Josephsgeschichte und ältere Chokma', *Congress Volume. Copenhagen 1953* (VT Suppl. 1), Leiden 1953, pp. 120–7 = *Gesammelte Studien zum alten Testament*, Munich, 1958, pp. 272–80.

fundamentally distinct—though not, as later developments show, ultimately incompatible—views about the way in which Israel ought to think of itself and live its national life. The standpoint of wisdom—both the native Israelite wisdom and the new court and didactic wisdom which, under foreign influence, had reached a clearer understanding of its own presuppositions—was by no means opposed to religion but was based on human reason and so was basically anthropocentric rather than theocentric. Its literature is directed mainly towards the individual, but its principles were applied by the wise men to the administration of the State and the formulation of national policy. It was here that the prophets joined issue with the wise men. The cause of the frequent clashes between the prophets and the kings of Judah and their advisers was the prophets' insistence that political decisions must be subservient to the instructions of Yahweh made known through the prophetic word. Politics and foreign policy must not be left to human ingenuity but belonged, like everything else, to God.[1] This theme runs right through the recorded oracles of Isaiah and Jeremiah. It is a condemnation of the king's political advisers, the men who had received their education in the wisdom schools, and who are referred to as a distinct class in Jer. 9.23; 18.18, and perhaps, under the name of 'elders', in Ezek. 7.26. Of the passages in Isaiah and Jeremiah in which those who consider themselves to be wise are condemned, it may be admitted that some (Isa. 5.21; Jer. 4.22) are not condemnations of a specific class but have a wider reference. But in at least three passages (Isa. 29.13–15; Jer. 9.23f.; 18.18) the reference is quite precise, and accords with the many other passages in which those who take political decisions are condemned by the prophets for basing those decisions on their own political judgment rather than on the instructions of Yahweh.

Yet on the other hand there are signs that the way of thinking represented by wisdom was already firmly established in Israel, and had even made inroads on the thinking of the prophets themselves. It has recently been pointed out[2] that there are a number of

---

[1] The two standpoints can be seen very clearly in such passages as the story of the confrontation of Isaiah and Ahaz in Isa. 7.1–17.
[2] Lindblom, *op. cit.*, and also J. Lindblom, *Prophecy in Ancient Israel*, Oxford, 1962 (see references in Index to 'Wisdom, Wisdom schools').

clear instances in both Isaiah and Jeremiah of the use of the style and vocabulary, and even of the teaching of the wise.[1]

More significantly there are signs in the teaching of these prophets that a *modus vivendi* between the two points of view was being sought. The basic formula for this is given in Isa. 31.2: 'yet he also is wise'. The idea that the source of wisdom is divine can hardly have been new to Israel. It was universally recognized throughout the ancient near east that this was so. In particular, this divinely bestowed wisdom was believed to be a special characteristic of kings, and the ascription of wisdom to Solomon was in keeping with this tradition. The statement in Isa. 11.2 that Yahweh will confer the spirit of wisdom on the ideal king is a further example of this belief. But in general wisdom was not one of the divine qualities stressed in the older Yahwistic tradition, nor in the prophets, for whom Yahweh was primarily a god of holiness, power, love, mercy, wrath, righteousness and judgment. Thus the few passages in which Isaiah and Jeremiah emphasize the wisdom of Yahweh (Isa. 28.29; 31.2; Jer. 10.12; cf. Isa. 5.21; 29.13-15; Jer. 4.22; 17.5-11) probably indicate that the confrontation of the prophets and the wise men was not merely negative in its results, but gave rise to an attempt by the prophets to grapple with the theological problem which the claims of the wise men had set them, and that in this way the Israelite concept of Yahweh was already beginning to be influenced by wisdom. If this is so, the occasional use by these prophets of words and ideas borrowed from the wisdom tradition is more easily understood.

It might be expected that the various traditions about Solomon's wisdom in I Kings[2] would provide further clues about this development, since at least three distinct concepts of wisdom are discernible here.[3] Unfortunately, however, the literary analysis and dating of these passages remain obscure.[4]

If there are signs that some of the pre-exilic prophets had begun to come to terms with the wisdom tradition by asserting that true

[1] Isa. 28.23-39; Jer. 17.5-11.
[2] 3.5-15, 16-28; 4.29-34 (Heb. 5.9-14); 10.1-13.
[3] Scott, *op. cit.*
[4] On this see Scott, *op. cit.*, and J. A. Montgomery, *A Critical and Exegetical Commentary on the Books of Kings* (ICC), 1951, *ad loc.*, especially pp. 105-8, and the literature referred to there.

wisdom is not the product of an independent human reason but rather a gift bestowed on men by Yahweh, one might also expect to find signs in the wisdom literature itself of such a *rapprochement*: signs that the custodians of Israelite wisdom realized from their side the desirability of bringing their teaching into more positive conformity with Israel's religious tradition. It has been maintained that there are such indications in Prov. 10–29. But the task of estimating the extent of the influence of specifically Yahwistic ideas in these chapters is not a simple one. It is clear that their authors were not slavish imitators of their foreign models, and that they were aware of the necessity of adapting their teaching to suit the needs of their Israelite readers. Even Prov. 22.17–23.11 is by no means simply a translation of *Amen-em-opet*. The setting is Israelite rather than Egyptian,[1] and it is specifically stated that it is Yahweh who protects and avenges the oppressed (22.23). In every section of Prov. 10–29 reference is made to Yahweh in similar terms, though in some sections his role is emphasized more than in others.[2] Moreover, these authors were selective in their use of foreign material. While the statement in Prov. 16.2 that 'Yahweh weigheth the spirits' probably shows that the author was familiar with the Egyptian belief that a man's heart is weighed before Osiris at the judgment after death, the Egyptian doctrine of the after-life, which was a very prominent feature of Egyptian religious belief and appears fairly frequently in Egyptian wisdom literature, has no place in Proverbs with this single exception, which may be a slip.

Yet the mere use of the name of Yahweh rather than that of some other god, and the omission of references to Egyptian beliefs which were incompatible with Israelite religion are not sufficient in themselves to show that the teaching of these collections is deeply influenced by the Yahwistic tradition. More positive evidence is required. The problem of the religion of Proverbs is fraught with difficulties. It cannot be denied that there is a religious element in the book. But it may be questioned how far this may be called the religion of Israel. The older view that these authors simply added a religious element, derived from the religious tradition of Israel, to a wholly or mainly secular material

[1] E.g. the reference to the 'gate' in 22.22 and to Sheol in 23.14.
[2] See Skladny, *op. cit.*

derived from their foreign models[1] is no longer tenable. For example, it is now recognized that a moral and religious attitude towards life is already discernible in the Egyptian wisdom books, not only in the relatively late *Amen-em-opet* and *Papyrus Insinger*[2] but also in the very earliest instructions.[3] It is therefore necessary to enquire whether the religion of Proverbs, apart from such superficial features as the use of the name of Yahweh, is characteristically Israelite, or whether it more closely resembles that of the wisdom teachers of Egypt or elsewhere.

Opinions on this question are divided. Gressmann and Sellin[4] spoke of the religion of Proverbs as being fundamentally different from that of Israel, and other writers have remarked that Proverbs shows no sign of familiarity with either the prophetic or the priestly tradition.[5] On the other hand, Gese and Skladny[6] both conclude that strong Yahwistic elements are present there, though Gese speaks of the assimilation of two traditions, while Skladny maintains that they stand side by side in a paradoxical manner. A distinction is made by many writers between Prov. 1–9 and the rest of the book, chapters 1–9 being held to be the latest part of Proverbs and deeply influenced by the religion of Israel.[7]

None of these writers, however, denies that the religion of Proverbs has distinctive features which are not found in the Yahwistic tradition, and none denies the similarity of these

[1] E.g. O. S. Rankin, *Israel's Wisdom Literature: Its Bearing on Theology and the History of Religion*, Edinburgh, 1936, p. 9.

[2] Translations in F. Lexa, *Papyrus Insinger: Les Enseignements Moraux d'un Scribe Égyptien du Premier Siècle après J.-C.*, Paris, 1926, and A. Volten, *Das Demotische Weisheitsbuch* (Analecta Aegyptiaca 2), Copenhagen, 1941.

[3] A. de Buck, 'Het religeus Karakter der oudste egyptische Wijsheid', *NTT* 21, 1932, pp. 322–49; H. Frankfort, *Ancient Egyptian Religion: An Interpretation*, New York, 1948; Brunner, *Erziehung*, pp. 116–23; H. Brunner, 'Die Weisheitsliteratur', *Handbuch der Orientalistik*, ed. B. Spuler, I, Leiden, 1952, p. 95; H. Gese, *Lehre und Wirklichkeit in der alten Weisheit*, Tübingen, 1958, pp. 27f.; E. Würthwein, *Die Weisheit Ägyptens und das Alte Testament*, Marburg, 1960, pp. 6–8, *et al.*

[4] H. Gressmann, *Israels Spruchweisheit im Zusammenhang der Weltliteratur* (Kunst und Altertum 6), Berlin, 1925, p. 53; E. Sellin, *Alttestamentliche Theologie auf religionsgeschichtlicher Grundlage* I, Leipzig, 1933, p. 116.

[5] E.g. H. Duesberg and P. Auvray, *Le Livre des Proverbes (SBJ)*, Paris, 1957, p. 11; Würthwein, *op. cit.*, pp. 8–11.

[6] *Lehre und Wirklichkeit* and *Die ältesten Spruchsammlungen*.

[7] On the relationship between Prov. 1–9 and the other books of the O.T. see especially A. Robert, 'Les attaches littéraires bibliques de Prov. I–IX', *RB* 43, 1934, pp. 42–68, 172–204, 374–84; 44, 1935, pp. 344–65, 502–25.

features to non-Israelite wisdom literature. The absence of reference to the cult, which is sufficient in itself to indicate a standpoint different from that of the other books of the Old Testament, is reminiscent of Egyptian wisdom.[1] The view of God is also distinctive: we find here not the dynamic God of the Old Testament tradition, but a remote sovereign who judges but does not interfere with human conduct. Indeed, as in Egyptian wisdom literature, the centre of interest is not God, but man; the motive, a successful and prosperous life (though morality is one of the necessary means to this, and traditional piety—since there is no word of opposition to it—is no doubt taken for granted). This anthropocentricity is not irreligious: there is no conflict between the demands of God and man's interests.

In all these and in other ways there is a basic community of thought between Proverbs and the Egyptian instructions. In ethical matters the contents of Proverbs frequently coincide with the prescriptions of the Old Testament laws and the teaching of the prophets, but while there may have been some direct influence here[2] the majority of points of resemblance are points on which most ethical codes agree. The similarities to Egyptian—and occasionally Mesopotamian—admonitions are both clearer and more numerous. This is also true of the motives. Nowhere else in the Old Testament do ethical demands occur without some reference, actual or implied, to the Covenant, or to the holiness or righteousness of Yahweh who makes these demands.

We may then reasonably infer that, while there are indications that in the pre-exilic period there was some interaction between the Yahwistic tradition, as represented by the prophets, and the wisdom teachers, in which lay the seeds of the eventual growing together of the two, the process was far from complete. The fundamental presuppositions of the two traditions still remained far apart. Nor, so far, has the study of Proverbs greatly contributed to an understanding of the stages by which this growing together took place, or of the part—if any—played in the process by the personification of wisdom in Prov. 1–9. Recent attempts to

---

[1] Admonitions to perform religious duties are not entirely absent from Egyptian wisdom literature, but they lie very much in the background.

[2] See Robert, *art. cit.* Many of his parallels, however, are no more than superficial resemblances, or merely indicative of a common Hebrew vocabulary.

Proverbs 1–9 and the Problem of Wisdom

distinguish between the points of view of the four sections of Prov. 10–29 and to arrange them in chronological order[1] have not been entirely convincing. The only universally accepted conclusion about relative dating is that 1–9 is later than the rest of the book; but this section is usually held to have been written after the assimilation of the two traditions was virtually completed, so that if this hypothesis is accepted we are still left with a great gap between 10–29 and 1–9. One of the main difficulties is the amorphous nature of the material in 10–29, which makes it very difficult to draw precise conclusions about the character of these sections. The almost universal unit is the single proverb; and, with a few exceptions, there appears to be no principle of arrangement. Sometimes two proverbs which appear to contradict one another are set side by side. The theory of a 'religious' and a 'secular' school of wisdom teachers whose proverbs have been mixed together,[2] which was formerly widely held, is now untenable in view of our increased knowledge of the general character of wisdom thought, and all attempts at detailed literary analysis have proved unsatisfactory owing to the large number of small units with no connecting links between them. Prov. 10–29 may well be the deposit of a long period of development, but the very form of the material has so far defeated all attempts at analysis.

The other two Old Testament wisdom books—Job and Ecclesiastes—offer little help towards the solution of the problem. While Proverbs, like its Egyptian models and its late successor Ecclesiasticus, is a didactic work bearing the mark of the wisdom school, Job and Ecclesiastes belong rather to the other type of wisdom literature which also had its models in Egypt and Mesopotamia: the reflective or meditative type. They do not stand in the same line of development, and they differ from the didactic books in intention, form and contents. The didactic works do not argue, nor do they seek to provoke thought or to resolve doubts. Their teaching is positive and authoritative. Job and Ecclesiastes, on the other hand, are attempts to communicate to the reader certain doubts and difficulties inherent in human existence, human society and man's relationship to God. They invite the reader to

[1] Such as that of Skladny, *op. cit.*
[2] E.g. R. H. Pfeiffer, *Introduction to the Old Testament*, New York, 1948, pp. 649ff.

reflect rather than to act. They both, in varying degrees, express criticism of the kind of teaching which Proverbs offers, and in doing so they depart from the main line of didactic wisdom teaching. Ecclesiasticus, coming at the end of this line, has obvious affinities with Proverbs, but shows no awareness of the problems which concern the authors of Job and Ecclesiastes.

Thus the problems remain, at present, without a satisfactory answer: by what means, and by what stages, did the great change in the concept of wisdom take place which is revealed by a comparison of Proverbs 10–29 and Ecclesiasticus? How was the full reconciliation of wisdom and the Yahwistic tradition achieved? And what was the role played in this process by the personification of wisdom in certain passages in Prov. 1–9? Although we have no positive evidence, we may presume that the destruction of the Jewish state in 587 had a profound effect on the development of the wisdom tradition. With the loss of the state, the *sōpᵉrim* lost their *raison d'être* as a distinct class, and its members found themselves living in Babylonia. There it is evident that they and their descendants kept the wisdom tradition alive. There they doubtless came into contact with Babylonian and Persian scribes. In Exile and Dispersion some Jews, of whom Nehemiah was one, attained positions of importance in the public service, such as probably required scribal qualifications. The case of Ezra is clearer: he is described in the decree of Artaxerxes (Ezra 7.12) as being both a scribe and a priest. In spite of the Chronicler's interpretation of the meaning of the word 'scribe' here in the later Jewish sense of 'skilled in the Law of Moses' (Ezra 7.6, 11), it is now believed[1] that it has the same sense as in earlier times: that is, Ezra belonged to the class of government officials who had received scribal training, and was in the service of the Persian Government. If Ezra 7.25 may be accepted, as is done by some scholars, as part of a genuine decree in which Artaxerxes gave Ezra his commission, we must conclude from it that by Ezra's time (roughly the beginning of the fourth century BC) the 'judaizing' of wisdom was already complete, for the phrase 'the wisdom of thy God which

---

[1] M. Noth, *The History of Israel*, 2nd ed., London, 1960, pp. 331f.; J. Bright, *A History of Israel*, London, 1960, pp. 369f. This interpretation was first fully expounded by H. H. Schaeder, *Esra der Schreiber*, Tübingen, 1930, pp. 39–59.

is in thy hand' certainly has the same meaning as 'the law of thy God which is in thy hand' in 7.14, that is, the Law of Moses.[1] In that case we should have a *terminus ad quem*, much earlier than the date of Ecclesiasticus, for the completion of the process. If, however, the latter part of the decree is held to be the work of the Chronicler,[2] we must accept a later date for this, though one which is still well before Ecclesiasticus; and for the time of Ezra we can merely note that the 'father of Judaism' was a scribe who may be presumed to have been versed equally in wisdom and in the Law of Moses.

The harsh experiences of exile and dispersion and the task of building a new Jewish community able to withstand the pressures of the outside world undoubtedly had a unifying effect on the Jews, and it was therefore natural that, under the new kind of leadership which arose at that time, the two traditions should have drawn closer together. But wherever we turn, we are merely presented with a *fait accompli*.

It is in the context of this very incomplete knowledge of the history of wisdom in Israel that we return to a re-examination of Prov. 1–9. It is a remarkable fact that these chapters have never been systematically studied as a possible source of information concerning the development of wisdom, although it is obvious that several distinct concepts of wisdom are to be found here. There have, it is true, been innumerable detailed studies of the background of 8.22–31, either in isolation or in relation to the other passages in which wisdom is personified or to the figure of the 'strange woman' or 'folly'. But insufficient attention has been paid in the past to the internal literary and theological problems of these chapters as a whole.[3] Most commentators have treated them

---

[1] The unresolved question, how much of the present Pentateuch was contained in the 'law' which Ezra took to Jerusalem does not affect the present argument.

[2] As by K. Galling, *Die Bücher der Chronik, Esra, Nehemia* (ATD 12), Göttingen, 1954, *ad loc.*

[3] The question was raised by some nineteenth-century commentators (so C. H. Toy, *Proverbs* [ICC], 1898, p. xxviii). Toy himself disagreed with the view that there are here two distinct views of wisdom, the one 'philosophical and speculative', the other 'hortatory and practical', but admitted that a few passages—such as 2.5–8—are additions made to correct the teaching of the immediately preceding verses. Since Toy, apart from a very widely

as a literary unity composed after the Exile. Yet the very divergent views which have been expressed about their place in the life of post-exilic Judaism are indicative of the difficulties involved in treating them as a unity. On the one hand the assertion in 1.7 that 'the fear of Yahweh is the beginning of knowledge' has been treated as a kind of slogan asserting that wisdom and the religion of Yahweh have now been recognized as being one and the same thing, and passages like 8.22–31 and 3.19f. have been taken to be fuller statements of this. Yet on the other hand their lack of interest in the main preoccupations of orthodox post-exilic Judaism—the Law and the cult—has led many interpreters to emphasize the radical difference between the standpoint of these chapters and that of Ecclesiasticus, and its similarity to that of the earlier wisdom collections of chapters 10–29.[1] Thus if they are to be dated after the Exile they must, on this view, be considered as deliberately ignoring, or even opposing, the legal reforms of Ezra and Nehemiah and the new Jewish community which they established, and so remaining apart from the main stream of Jewish life.[2] The difficulty of reconciling these apparently mutually

---

held opinion that two passages—6.1–19 and 9.7–12—are interpolations of a quite different kind of wisdom literature, only two writers have taken seriously the view that there are serious internal theological disagreements. L. Finkelstein, *The Pharisees: the Sociological Background of their Faith* I, Philadelphia, 1938, pp. 203–16, argued that the chapters as a whole constitute an educational discourse written for patrician youth in the hellenistic period, to which a Hasidean editor has made more religious but plebeian additions (he cites 1.5a; 3.5–12 as examples). On the other hand, Oesterley, Westminster Commentary, 1929, p. xiii, maintained that older, worldly and prudential passages were incorporated by a later, more religious writer into his own work! Neither of these two scholars, however, made a systematic analysis of the whole of these chapters. Other writers (e.g. W. F. Albright, *From the Stone Age to Christianity*, Baltimore, 1940, p. 283) have stated that all or part of chapters 8 and 9 differs in authorship from chapters 1–7, but again without offering detailed justification of their views. Most of the other commentaries, Introductions and other studies passed over the problem in silence, though a few (e.g. S. R. Driver, *Introduction to the Old Testament*, 9th ed., Edinburgh, 1913; H. Duesberg and P. Auvray, *SBJ*, 1957; R. H. Pfeiffer, *Introduction to the Old Testament*, New York, 1941) strongly maintained unity of authorship.

[1] E.g. J. Fichtner, *Die altorientalische Weisheit in ihrer israelitisch-jüdischen Ausprägung: eine Studie zur Nationalisierung der Weisheit in Israel* (BZAW 62), Giessen, 1933, pp. 124–8; J. C. Rylaarsdam, *Revelation in Jewish Wisdom Literature*, Chicago, 1946, pp. 18–26.

[2] So Sellin, *op. cit.*, pp. 115f.; H. Ranston, *The Old Testament Wisdom Books and Their Teaching*, London, 1930, pp. 14–17.

incompatible standpoints has led to such radical theories as that of Causse, who assigned the authorship of almost all Israel's wisdom literature, including these chapters, to the Jews of the pre-hellenistic Dispersion in Egypt, about whom we know very little, but who may have combined a freedom from the legalism of Ezra with a desire to convert the Egyptians by demonstrating the compatibility of their wisdom with the worship of Yahweh.[1]

These difficulties arise from certain inconsistencies in the thought of these chapters, and disappear once it is recognized that they are in fact not a literary unity at all. Of this there are some quite obvious indications. The material is quite different from that in the collections in chapters 10–29. Here are no collections of unrelated proverbs: on the contrary, we have a series of relatively lengthy sections in each of which there is a sustained continuity of thought. There is therefore full opportunity for a critical examination of the literary structure and the thought of these chapters along two well-tried lines of Old Testament literary criticism: the study of the relation of each section to the others, and the examination of the internal structure of each section. With regard to the first, it is immediately obvious that there are two main types of passage: that in which the wisdom teacher addresses his pupil and offers his own human teaching as the model to be followed, and that in which a personified wisdom, claiming to possess a plenitude of divine authority, makes a direct appeal to men. In other words, there is more than one concept of wisdom here. With regard to the second line of enquiry, the grammatical complexities and shifting emphases within some of the sections (ch. 2 is an obvious example) immediately give rise to the suspicion that relatively homogeneous short passages have been expanded by later hands. Thus in these chapters—and nowhere else in Proverbs—we are offered the fascinating possibility that a study of their literary history may enable us to discern with some precision the existence of more than one stage in the development of wisdom in Israel and the relations of these stages to one

[1] A. Causse, 'L'Origine Etrangère et la Tendance humaniste de la Sagesse juive', *Actes du Congrès d'Histoire des Religions* II, Paris, 1925, pp. 45–54; 'La Sagesse et la propagande juive à l'époque perse et hellénistique', *Werden und Wesen des alten Testaments*, ed. P. Volz and F. Stummer, Berlin, 1936, pp. 148–54; 'Sagesse égyptienne et sagesse juive', *RHPR* 1929, pp. 149–69.

another, and so to gain an insight into the history of that development and the reasons for it. If such an investigation can be successfully carried out, it may be possible to understand the relation of 8.22–31 and similar passages to their contexts, and so to come closer to an understanding of the meaning and purpose of the enigmatic figure of wisdom.

II

THE BOOK OF THE TEN DISCOURSES

THOSE parts of Prov. 1–9 in which it is the human wisdom teacher and not wisdom herself who speaks consist of a preface (1.1ff.) and ten originally independent speeches, which we shall call 'discourses', each preceded by its own introduction in which a 'father' (i.e. instructor) exhorts his 'son' (i.e. pupil) to pay attention to his words and points out the advantages which will accrue from doing so. These introductory formulae occur at 1.8ff.; 2.1ff.; 3.1ff.; 3.21ff.; 4.1ff.; 4.10ff.; 4.20ff.; 5.1ff.; 6.20ff.; 7.1ff.[1] Their length and contents vary considerably, but a comparison reveals that they are derived from a common basic form, which in some cases has been expanded by additions which introduce new and originally extraneous ideas.[2] The original form can be clearly seen in 1.8f.:

> My son, hear the instruction of thy father,
> And forsake not the teaching of thy mother:
> For they shall be a fair garland for thy head,
> And necklaces for thy neck.

Three others (3.1–4; 4.20–22; 5.1f.) have also preserved virtually their original form. The other six have all been expanded either

---

[1] Three other passages (5.7; 6.1; 7.24) resemble the ten introductions in some ways, but must be excluded from the list. 5.7 and 7.24, which are identical, are shorter than the introductions and occur not at the beginning but in the middle of blocks of teaching. The word 'my son' in 6.1 stands at the head of a new section, but this section (6.1–19) is rightly held by many commentators to be an independent collection of proverbs which had no place in the original book. See further, e.g., Gemser, *ad loc.* Other occurrences of 'my son' (1.10, 15; 3.11, etc.) are merely parenthetical.

[2] The method of using the introductory formulae as a criterion for distinguishing separate discourses is not new, but has never previously been consistently applied. F. Delitzsch (*Das Salomonische Spruchbuch*, Leipzig, 1873) distinguished 15 '*Spruchrede*' partly on this basis, and G. Wildeboer (*Sprüche* [KHAT], 1898), following earlier work by A. Kamphausen, showed a greater appreciation of the importance of the formulae with his 7 '*Abschnitte*', each

internally or by additions at the end, but in every case the original formula can be discerned: 2.1, 9; 3.21-24; 4.1f.; 4.10-12; 6.20-22; 7.1-3. There are differences of language and metaphor, but all have the following common characteristics:

1. They all begin with the word 'my son' (4.1 'sons').
2. They all command the pupil to 'hear', 'receive', 'not forget', etc., the instruction which follows. (The conditional form of 2.1ff. has the same force as the imperative of the others.)

---

of which begins with an introduction or '*Überschrift*'. He also, however, was not consistent: six of his introductions correspond to those used in the present analysis, but he failed to recognize three others of precisely the same type (3.21ff.; 4.10ff.; 4.20ff.), and also rather surprisingly included 8.1, which, although it clearly marks the beginning of a new section, bears no resemblance to the others. His method was essentially correct, however, and it is unfortunate that it was abandoned by later scholars just at the time when the foreign material then becoming known would have confirmed its correctness.

Since the beginning of this century the opinion of S. R. Driver (*op. cit.*, p. 395) that in Prov. 1-9 'no definite arrangement can be traced in the subjects treated' (cf. the similar comment, a generation later, of van der Ploeg, *Spreuken* [BOT], 1952, pp. 10f.) seems to have prevailed, and to have inhibited serious attempts at literary analysis, either on the assumption of unity of authorship or in terms of literary development. Some commentators (e.g. van der Ploeg and Duesberg and Auvray) regarded the whole of these chapters as constituting a single extended speech by a teacher to his pupil in which no structure is to be looked for; the majority, including Cohen, Gemser (the most important of the modern commentators), Hamp, Oesterley and Renard, were content to divide the chapters into convenient sections mainly according to the sense without attempting to find either an original or a superimposed structure in the material as a whole. Pfeiffer (*op. cit.*, p. 647), following an earlier theory of H. L. Strack, claimed that in the central section, chapters 3-7 are an elaboration of themes first announced in chapter 2; but he paid no attention to form, and his argument is forced. Eissfeldt (*Einleitung in das Alte Testament*, Tübingen, 1934, pp. 581ff.; cf. Engl. [1965] of 3rd ed.) held that these chapters are a collection of short poems, but like most other writers did not recognize the structural importance of the introductory formulae, and did not attempt to distinguish larger units (e.g. one of his short poems consists merely of 1.8f., which is, in fact, an introductory formula). Gemser's divisions sometimes straddle the introductory formulae: e.g. 3.13-26.

The only writer who fully grasped the significance of the formulae was Klostermann (*art. cit.* in *Theol. Studien Th. Zahn*, pp. 203f.). He rightly perceived that their almost identical wording indicates that each introduces an originally independent composition, and suggested that these were homiletic discourses used by the wisdom teacher before or after more detailed practical instruction to stimulate the emotions and wills of the pupils in a fatherly way so that they should take his teaching to heart. Klostermann did not, however, work out his theory in detail, and it has not been followed up since.

The Book of the Ten Discourses

3. They all assert the personal authority of the teacher. (Note the frequency of the pronominal suffix 'my'.)[1]

4. They all assert or imply the great value and utility of the teacher's words. This is expressed in various ways: their observance confers a long and happy life (3.2, 22; 4.10, 22; 7.2); they are a guide through the difficulties of life (3.23f.; 6.22); they beautify the person who observes them (1.9; 3.22); they are identified with understanding, sound wisdom, discretion, etc.; they are to be kept in the heart as a treasure, etc. (2.2; 4.21; 6.21; 7.3).

5. There is no reference whatever to any authority beyond that of the teacher himself. (The single reference to God, 3.4, is not a reference to divine authority: the words 'God and man' are no more than a set phrase indicating universality—cf. Judg. 9.13.)

6. In distinction from many other passages in Prov. 1–9, the word 'wisdom', which only occurs twice (5.1; 4.11), means ordinary human wisdom, and is not treated as a word of any special significance. The teacher calls it 'my wisdom' (5.1) and equates it with 'understanding' ($t^eb\bar{u}n\bar{a}$, 5.1) and 'virtue' ($y\bar{o}\check{s}er$, 4.11). No claim to divine inspiration is made, nor is wisdom in any way personified.[2]

These introductions, similar in form and content and of roughly equal length, so strongly resemble the introductions to the pedagogical instructions in Egyptian (and to some extent Babylonian) wisdom literature that the resemblance can hardly be accidental. The closest parallel is with *Amen-em-opet*, which also has the form of the instructions of a father to his son; but there are also many parallels with the introductions to other works, sufficient to make it clear that the author of these Israelite discourses was following a well-established pattern.[3] Some of these

---

[1] In 3.21 the 'my' is preserved only in LXX. Heb. must be incorrect as it stands, since there is no antecedent in the previous verses for the plural verb 'let them not depart'. The original text is probably to be obtained by reversing the two halves of the verse and adding the suffix 'my' to both nouns in v. 21b. If this is done, the formula fits the pattern of the others.

[2] For a justification of the excision of 2.2–8, 10f.; 4.5–9; 4.13; 7.4, where such claims are made, see pp. 40ff., *infra*.

[3] Especially the *Instruction of King Amenemhēt* (Erman, p. 72, and *ANET*, p. 418); the *Instruction of Sehetepibrē* (Erman, p. 84); an anonymous instruction of a father to his son (Brunner, *Erziehung*, p. 161); the *Instruction of Amennakht* (Brunner, p. 179); the *Wisdom of Anii* (Erman, p. 235); the Sumero-Accadian *Instructions of Šuruppak* (W. G. Lambert, *Babylonian Wisdom Literature*, Oxford, 1960, p. 93); a Sumero-Accadian dialogue between master and pupil quoted in G. R. Driver, *Semitic Writing from Pictograph to Alphabet* (Schweich Lectures, 1944), London, 1948, pp. 65f. For the contents compare also the epilogue to the *Instruction of Ptahhotep* (Erman, pp. 63–65).

Wisdom in Proverbs

parallels are so close as to be almost verbally identical.[1] The meaning of the command to 'hear', which is the main feature of the introductions, is the same as in the Egyptian instructions, where 'hearing' is much more than a simple action and has acquired the sense of the whole attitude towards life which the teacher wants to inculcate in his pupil.[2]

The similarity between the first chapter of *Amen-em-opet* and our material is apparent even at the first glance. The former begins thus:

> Give thine ears, hear (the words) that are said,
>   Give thy mind to interpret them;
> To put them in thy heart is good,
>   (But there is) woe to him that neglecteth them.
> Let them rest in the casket of thy belly,
>   That they may be the threshold (?) in thy heart;
> Verily (?) when there cometh a gale of speech,
>   They will be a mooring-post (?) in thy tongue.
> If thou spend thy life-time with these things in thy heart,
>   Thou wilt find it a success;
> Thou wilt find my words a storehouse of life
>   And thy body will prosper upon earth.[3]

Amen-em-opet with its thirty chapters is on a much larger scale than the discourses in Proverbs, and its introduction also is, accordingly, longer; but, allowing for differences of metaphor and style, the similarities are remarkable: in both we have the idea of guarding the teaching in the heart, and the list of benefits which accrue from following the teaching: long life, health, prosperity and freedom from difficulties. Even the image of the path of life (Prov. 3.23; 4.11f.) occurs in *Amen-em-opet*, though not in the same chapter.[4]

---

[1] E.g. the double command, positive and negative, which is characteristic of the introduction in Proverbs (4.20f., 'My son, be attentive to my words . . . let them not escape from thy sight'; cf. 1.8; 3.21;6.20) is extremely close to the 'Be attentive and listen to my words, neglect not what I say' of *Amennakht* and many other Egyptian introductions.

[2] See esp. *Ptahhotep* (Erman, pp. 63–65).

[3] *Amen-em-opet* I, 3.9–4.2. (In this and the following references to *Amen-em-opet* Roman figures refer to the chapter and Arabic numerals to column and line.)

[4] It occurs in the general preface to the book (1.7): 'To direct him to the path of life', and is also found elsewhere in Egyptian wisdom literature.

The Book of the Ten Discourses

Attempts have been made to demonstrate that the author of the discourses derived his terminology rather from biblical sources (especially Deuteronomy, and to a lesser extent Isaiah and Jeremiah) than from foreign wisdom instructions.[1] But while there may be biblical reminiscences in a few cases,[2] the parallels with *Amen-em-opet* are in general much closer than the biblical parallels. It is true that such phrases as 'teach' (*hōrā*), 'teaching' (*tōrā*), 'do not forget', 'attend', etc., occur also in Deuteronomy, but these are merely the common vocabulary of education in Hebrew and do not prove any direct influence. Moreover, the whole context is different from that of the pedagogical passages in Deuteronomy and other biblical books. Whereas the latter are addressed to Israel as a whole in the context of the covenant, the discourses are addressed to an individual or a small group of pupils and make no reference to Israel or to Yahweh. In the one case the teaching is proclaimed on the authority of Yahweh; in the latter on the purely human authority of the wisdom teacher. There can be no doubt that the discourses in Proverbs 1–9 stand firmly in the tradition of international wisdom and are not derived from, though they may have been to some extent influenced by, the Yahwistic tradition.[3]

THE TEN DISCOURSES[4]

The Preface

1.1 The Proverbs of Solomon the son of David king of Israel,
  2 For knowing wisdom and instruction,
    For comprehending words of understanding;

---

[1] Especially Robert, *art. cit.*, RB, 43–44.
[2] The command to 'bind' (*qāšar*) the teacher's instruction on the heart, neck or fingers (Prov. 3.3; 6.21; 7.3) and to write them on the heart, which have no true parallels in *Amen-em-opet* or the other Egyptian instructions, may be reminiscences of Deut. 6.4–9, where the Israelites are commanded to bind (*qāšar*) Yahweh's words on the hand and forehead, and to write them on the gates of their houses. Ex. 13.9, 16; Jer. 17.1; 31.33, also use a similar metaphor.
[3] See especially P. Humbert, *Recherches sur les sources égyptiennes de la littérature sapientiale d'Israël*, Neuchâtel, 1929, pp. 34ff.
[4] Agreements and disagreements with earlier studies regarding the literary analysis of the material are indicated as often as possible in the notes. For further details see the commentaries.

3 For receiving instruction in prudence,
   Righteousness, justice and right conduct;
4 For giving to the inexperienced shrewdness,
   To the young man knowledge and discretion.
5 Let the wise man hearken and increase his instruction,
   And the judicious man acquire guidance.[1]

In both form and content these verses correspond closely to the titles and prefaces of Egyptian and Mesopotamian instructions. The title (v. 1) is in accordance with the Egyptian custom of attributing wisdom instructions to kings.[2] For the other verses there is a very close parallel in the preface (not to be confused with the introduction, mentioned above) of *Amen-em-opet* (1.1–12):

Beginning of teaching how to live,
   Guidance for welfare;
Every direction for intercourse with elders,
   Rules for (intercourse with?) courtiers;
Knowledge how to answer a statement to its pronouncer,
   And return a report to one that has sent him;
To direct him to the path of life,
   And make him prosper upon earth;
To let his heart enter its shrine,
   And steer it clear of evil;
To save him from the mouth of others,
   Praised in the mouth of men.

Although the Egyptian preface states the aim of the instruction in a more detailed way than the Israelite preface, it is in both cases an educational one,[3] and the grammatical structure is the same. Moreover, in both cases there is the odd fact that a very impersonal

---

[1] V. 6, which speaks of technical skill rather than wisdom in the wider sense, does not belong to the original preface but was probably added when its scope was extended to include the whole of Proverbs. V. 7, whose purpose is to equate the wisdom of vv. 1–5 with the practice of Yahwism, is also a later addition. Its form (antithetical parallelism) is different from that of vv. 1–5. It equally clearly does not form part of the discourse which follows, as Oesterley, Gemser and van der Ploeg take it.

[2] The *Instruction for King Merikerē* (Erman, pp. 75–84; *ANET*, pp. 414–18); *Amenembēt* (Erman and *ANET*, loc. cit.). Cf. *Šuruppak* (Lambert, loc. cit.). See also P. Humbert, op. cit., p. 64.

[3] 'Welfare', 'the path of life', 'prospering on earth' and 'being steered clear of evil' are basically the same as 'knowing wisdom', 'comprehending words of understanding', etc.

The Book of the Ten Discourses

statement of purpose is prefixed to instructions which are very personal and addressed to a single pupil. There are also resemblances between Prov. 1.1–5 and the prefaces to other Egyptian instructions.[1]

Discourse I. The Avoidance of Evil Company

1.8 My son, hear the instruction of thy father,
And forsake not the teaching of thy mother:
9 For they shall be a fair garland for thy head,
And necklaces for thy neck.

10 My son, if sinners entice thee,
(Saying) 'Come with us', do not consent;
11 If they say, 'Let us lie in wait for the innocent,
Let us lie in ambush for the innocent with impunity;[2]
12 Like Sheol let us swallow them alive
And whole, like those who go down to the Pit;
13 All precious goods shall we find,
We shall fill our houses with spoil;
14 Throw in thy lot among us,
We shall all have one purse.'
15 My son, do not walk in the way with them,
Hold back thy foot from their path.[3]
17 For in vain is a net spread
In the sight of any bird;[4]
18 Yet these men lie in wait for their own blood,
They set an ambush for their own lives.
19 Such is the end[5] of every one who runs after profit:
It takes away the life of its possessors.

---

[1] Esp. *Ptahhotep* (Erman, p. 56, and *ANET*, *ad loc.*). Cf. also *Amen-em-opet* XXX, 27.7–17.

[2] The removal of 'Come with us' from 11a to 10b restores both verses to their proper length without impairing the sense. In 11a 'for the innocent' ($l^e tām$) gives a better parallel than MT $l^e dām$, 'for blood', though the emendation is purely conjectural.

[3] V. 16 is an interpolation taken from Isa. 59.7a and inserted here, perhaps to provide a more religious reason for the avoidance of sin. It is absent from the best MSS of LXX (except A).

[4] Adopting the emendation of *BH* as offering the most probable, though not certain, solution. But see D. W. Thomas, *Wisdom in Israel* (VT Suppl. 3), p. 281, for the problem and other possible solutions. The most probable interpretation is that the sinners are more stupid than the wily birds.

[5] Reading $'ah^a rit$ for $'or^e ḇōt$ ('paths') for the sake of the sense and following LXX. (So Toy, Gemser, Duesberg and Auvray, Renard.)

Discourse II. Avoidance of the 'Strange Woman'
2.1 My son, if thou wilt receive my words,
   And lay up my commandments with thee,
 9 Then shalt thou understand righteousness and justice,
   And right conduct—every path leading to good fortune.[1]

16 They will deliver thee[2] from the 'strange woman',
   From the 'stranger' with her smooth words,
17 Who forsakes the companion of her youth
   And has forgotten the covenant of her God;
18 For her house sinks down[3] to death,
   And her paths to the shades;
19 None who goes into her ever returns,
   Nor does he regain the paths of life.

A very large quantity of material has been added to this discourse. The above reconstruction of the original corresponds almost exactly to 5.1–6, where the original shape is clearly visible, since there additions have been made only at the end. Some commentators have attempted to discover a logical pattern of thought in the chapter as a whole,[4] but it abounds in difficult grammatical connexions and changes of subject.[5] It is also extremely repetitive: 'wisdom' and synonyms for wisdom occur nine times in vv. 1–11 and words for 'path' nine times in vv. 12–22;

---

[1] There is some doubt about the correctness of the text of 9b. No fully satisfactory alternative has been proposed. See, however, Toy, *ad loc.*
[2] The construction (*lᵉhaṣṣilᵉkā*) is very loose. Cf. 6.24; 7.5; 16.30; 18.24; 19.8; 30.14, and see G.-K. 114 i and note.
[3] The transfer of the accent of this word (*šāḥā*) from the first to the second syllable gives excellent sense and grammar and avoids emendation of the consonantal text which would otherwise be necessary to secure the agreement of the verb with the subject. On the verb *šāḥā* see G. R. Driver, *JTS* 31, 1929–30, p. 280.
[4] Wildeboer, Oesterley, Gemser, Renard. They divide it into six stanzas (vv. 1–4, 5–8, 9–11, 12–15, 16–19, 20–22) on metrical grounds, and interpret the last five of these as describing five blessings or consequences which flow from obedience to the instruction given in the first. While the metrical symmetry (whether by design or accident) is a fact, the argument that there are five distinct 'blessings' is difficult to follow.
[5] J. van der Ploeg, *Spreuken* (BOT), 1952, *ad loc.*, pointed out the lack of a clear structure, but attributed this to 'typical oriental' literary methods of composition. Others have regarded some verses as secondary: Toy, *ad loc.* (vv. 5–8, with v. 20 misplaced); L. Finkelstein, *The Pharisees: The Sociological Background of their Faith* I, pp. 205f. (vv. 2–8).

and the same thought is often wearisomely repeated. Verses 2–8, which greatly extend the scope of what the pupil is exhorted to acquire by identifying the teacher's words with wisdom conceived as a precious commodity and a divine gift, have been introduced into the original introductory formula by the device of adding additional, parallel protases and apodoses to the simple conditional sentence in vv. 1, 9. Similarly verses 10–15, which also speak of wisdom in a similar way, have been appended by means of an explanatory clause beginning with 'for' (*kī*, v. 10). Verses 20–22 are also clearly secondary. Verse 19 is the natural and dramatic conclusion to the discourse (cf. 7.27; 9.18); and v. 20 (which Toy wanted to transfer to after 9) makes no sense after it. Verses 21, 22 are statements of a general character, quite unlike the intimate and personal advice of the wisdom teacher in these discourses. It is possible that vv. 20–22 are a misplaced conclusion of the secondary section vv. 12–15; but they do not belong to the discourse which, shorn of all its secondary material, forms a concise and satisfactory unit, similar in form and content to 5.1–8, which has not been expanded by the addition of interpretative comment.[1]

Discourse III. Duties towards God

  3.1 My son, forget not my teaching,
      But let thy heart keep my commandments;
    2 For length of days and years of life
      And peace will they bring to thee.
   3b Bind them about thy neck;
    c Write them on the tablet of thy heart.[2]
    4 So shalt thou find favour and a good reputation[3]
      In the sight of God and man.

[1] See p. 47, *infra*.
[2] If one of the three stichoi of this verse is an interpolation, as is probable, it is the first one. Exhortations like 3bc are elsewhere (6.21; 7.3; cf. 1.9; 3.22) made with reference to the words of the wisdom teacher, and never refer to abstract qualities like loyalty and truth. With the omission of 3a, the introduction to this discourse has the same form as the other introductions. This consideration outweighs the significance of the fact that one MS. of LXX omits 3c rather than 3a, a solution adopted by several commentators (Oesterley, Gemser, Renard, Duesberg and Auvray) who regard 3c as a gloss, introduced in imitation of 7.3.
[3] For this meaning of *śēkel-ṭōb* see Gemser, *ad loc.* and cf. Prov. 13.15; Ps. 111.10.

Wisdom in Proverbs

5 Trust in Yahweh with all thy heart,
And rely not on thine own understanding.
6 In all thy ways consider him,
And he will make thy paths straight.
7 Be not wise in thine own sight;
Fear Yahweh, and turn away from evil.
8 That will be healing for thy flesh
And a medicament for thy bones.[1]
9 Honour Yahweh with thy wealth,
And with the first fruits of all thy produce:
10 Then thy barns will be filled with grain,[2]
And thy vats with new wine.

Of the verses which follow, 13–20 are secondary; 11f. probably so. The body of the discourse (vv. 5–10) consists of three admonitions of equal length, describing three duties to Yahweh. Verses 11f., beginning with the word 'my son', which usually marks the beginning of a new section, have a different structure, introduce a new concept of retribution,[3] and are concerned not with duties toward God but with man's reaction to God's actions toward him. They were probably added to meet objections (similar to those of Job) that right conduct does not, in fact, always lead to prosperity.

Verses 13–18 are a poem, beginning with the words *'ašrē 'ādām*, which (or their equivalent) are found elsewhere at the beginning of wisdom poems (Pss. 1.1; 32.1; 41.2; 112.1; 119.1; 128.1). They are not addressed to the pupil but are a general statement wholly concerned with wisdom, to which there is no reference in the

---

[1] *šōr* = 'navel' is unlikely in 8a. The word may be *šōr*, 'health' (Syriac *šrīrā*, see G. R. Driver, *Biblica* 32, p. 175; *Aramaic Documents*, Oxford, 1957, p. 44 and n. 2) or *šēr* (for *šeʾēr*), 'flesh' (Oort). In 8b *šiqqūy* may be a kind of ointment (cf. Driver, *Biblica, ibid.* and Hos. 2.7); and 'bones' has the meaning of 'bodily frame'.

[2] Most commentators, so interpreting LXX, emend *šābāʿ*, usually 'plenty', to *šeber*, 'grain', which gives better sense and parallelism. Emendation may not, however, be necessary to obtain the meaning 'grain', in view of Phoenician *šbʿ wtrš*, apparently 'grain and new wine', in the Karatepe Inscription. See M. Dahood, *Proverbs and Northwest Semitic Philology*, Rome, 1963, p. 9.

[3] I use this word simply to mean the relationship between conduct and reward, without giving it the special sense which it has received in modern debate (e.g. H. Gunkel, 'Vergeltung', *RGG*² *V*, col. 1532).

preceding verses.¹ Verses 19f. are again in a different style and are a poem or part of a poem about Yahweh's creation of the world by wisdom.²

Discourse IV. Duties towards One's Neighbour

3.21b My son, keep my sound wisdom and discretion,
    a Let them not escape from thy sight;³
22 They will be life for thy soul,
    And adornment for thy neck.
23 Then shalt thou walk securely on thy way,
    And thy foot shall not stumble.
24 If thou sittest down⁴ thou shalt not be afraid,
    And if thou liest down thy sleep will be sweet.⁵

27 Withhold not good from those to whom it is due⁶
    When it is in thy power to do it.
28 Say not to thy neighbour, 'Go, and come again,
    And tomorrow I will give it', when thou hast it with thee.
29 Plan not evil against thy neighbour,
    When he is living trustfully near thee.
30 Contend not against a man without a cause,
    If he has done thee no harm.
31 Envy not a man of violence,
    And choose not any of his ways.

It is not clear where this discourse ends. The admonitions (expressed in the singular imperative) end with v. 31, and each of

---

¹ For another such independent poem in praise of wisdom see Job 28, especially vv. 12–19. P. Volz (*Hiob und Weisheit*, Göttingen, 1921, pp. 144f.) treated Prov. 3.13–18 as a separate poem.

¹ For the literary relations of vv. 19f. see p. 99, *infra*.

³ See p. 35, n. 1 *supra*.

⁴ Reading *tēšēb* for *tiškab*, following LXX (so Toy, Gemser, Duesberg and Auvray, Renard). It is unlikely that the same verb should have been used in both clauses. Cf. also Deut. 6.7 *et al*.

⁵ Vv. 25f. are secondary. They merely repeat what has already been said in vv. 23f. and have been added to introduce Yahweh, rather than the wisdom of the teacher, as the ultimate source of protection from the vicissitudes of life. Most commentators are agreed that there is secondary material in vv. 25–35. Toy (followed by Oesterley and Gemser) recognized that vv. 27–30 are unrelated to their context, but, contrary to Toy's opinion, the form and contents of 27–31 (five short negative admonitions) show that it is just these verses, and not the generalizations of vv. 25f., 32–35, which are original.

⁶ Or possibly 'from those who seek it', reading *mibbōʿē lō* for *mibbeʿālāw* on the basis of LXX. It has been questioned whether *baʿal* can have the meaning given here; though cf. Accadian *bēl ḥubulli*, 'creditor'.

the following verses (32–35) is a general statement in the form of antithetical parallelism contrasting the fates of the wicked and the righteous, the wise and the fools, etc., in the manner of other collections in Proverbs. It is quite possible that the discourse originally ended with one or more such general statements (cf. 1.19, which, although not in antithetical form, is a general statement about the fate of the wicked), but a series of four completely general statements would be unique in these personal discourses, as will be shown in the discussion of the others. It is perhaps most likely that the discourse ended with v. 32, which is attached to the previous verse by the particle *kī* ('for'), and may be said to give a reason for the admonitions of the discourse as a whole:

> For the crooked man is an abomination to Yahweh,
> But his intimacy is with the upright.[1]

Discourse V. The Traditional Character of Wisdom

> 4.1 Hear, O sons, the instruction of a father,
> And be attentive, that you may gain understanding;
> 2 For I give you good precepts:
> Abandon not my teaching.
>
> 3 For I (also) was a weak child,
> An only one, in my father's care;[2]
> 4a And he taught me and said unto me,
> b 'Let thy heart hold fast my words;
> c Keep my commandments, (5ba) forget them not,
> 5bβ And turn not away from the words of my mouth.'[3]

This section (4.1–9) presents peculiar difficulties. If v. 5a is omitted as a gloss, v. 6 has no antecedent. To avoid this difficulty it has been proposed to transpose vv. 6 and 7.[4] However, 7a is

---

[1] Toy and Gemser held that vv. 31–35 are secondary, but did not recognize that the concrete nature of v. 31 distinguishes it from the verses which follow.

[2] Following the emendation of Toy except in one particular. The text as it stands is corrupt: the first part is a truism, and the reference to the mother in the second half is ignored by the singular 'and he taught me' in v. 4. Toy's change of *yāḥīd* to *yādīd*, however, is unnecessary and is not, as Toy maintains, necessarily supported by LXX's 'beloved', since LXX elsewhere (Gen. 22 *passim*; Amos 8.10 *et al.*) translates *yāḥīd* as 'beloved'.

[3] Omitting the last word of v. 4 and 5a with most MSS. of LXX. 5a is metrically redundant and is an anticipation of v. 7. So Gemser, *ad loc.*; cf. Oesterley.

[4] Gemser, *ad loc.*

The Book of the Ten Discourses

clearly corrupt. It is possible that some words have dropped out. It is, however, clear that vv. 6–9 are a secondary passage which has been added in order to identify the words of the teacher with wisdom, which is not mentioned in vv. 1–5.[1]

The contents of the discourse as reconstructed (vv. 1–5 minus 5a) are thus quite different from those of the other discourses so far considered. In place of the usual practical admonitions we have reminiscences of the teacher's own youth in which by implication the teacher commends his own youthful diligence as a model for his pupil to follow. It is not clear whether vv. 3–5 should be considered as part of the introduction to a discourse of which the main body is now missing, or whether, in spite of their differences from the other discourses, they are, in fact, the body of the discourse. There are close parallels to them in Egyptian wisdom literature,[2] although none in which such reminiscences form a whole chapter of an instruction.

Discourse VI. Avoidance of Evil Company

4.10 Hear, my son, and accept my words,
And the years of thy life shall be many.
11 In the way of wisdom do I guide thee,
I lead thee in the paths of virtue.
12 When thou walkest, thy step will not be cramped,
And when thou runnest, thou shalt not stumble.

14 Enter not the path of the wicked,
And walk not on the road of evil men.[3]
15 Avoid it, pass not along it,
Turn away from it, and pass on.
16 For they sleep not unless they have done wrong,
And their sleep escapes them unless they have assaulted someone.

---

[1] It is possible, however, that behind v. 9, which uses expressions elsewhere used of the teacher's instruction (1.9), lies an original verse of the same kind, which may have followed v. 5.

[2] Especially in the *Kemit*, a book of instruction for teachers from the Middle Kingdom: 'My father also trained me in the useful writings which had come down to him. Then I found that men praised me, since I had become wise (?), since my eyes had been opened' (Brunner, *Erziehung*, pp. 158f.; cf. also other similar examples on pp. 162ff.).

[3] Here it is necessary to read *tēʾšar* for the Piel *tᵉʾaššēr*, which elsewhere always has a causative sense. No consonantal emendation is necessary. (Toy.)

> 17 For they eat the bread of wickedness,
> And the wine of violence do they drink.
> 19 The way of the wicked is like darkness:
> They do not know over what they stumble.[1]
> 18 But the path of the righteous is like the morning light,
> Increasing in brightness until the day is full.[2]

The only secondary material in 4.10–19 is v. 13. It interrupts the continuity of thought, which in every other verse from v. 11 to v. 15 is expressed in metaphors derived from walking along a path. It is a gloss, and it is also probably corrupt, since the word *mūsār* ('instruction' or 'discipline'), though elsewhere always masculine, is here treated as feminine.[3] It is conceivable that the feminine noun *ḥokmā* originally stood here in place of *mūsār*; if so, the verse expresses the same thought as 3.18, the final verse of the poem on wisdom in 3.13–18.

With this exception, this discourse, the extent of which is determined by the next introductory formula in 4.20, may be taken as a good example of the discourses which formed the original material in these chapters.[4]

Discourse VII. The Importance of Vigilance

> 4.20 My son, be attentive to my words;
> Incline thine ear to my speech.
> 21 Let them not escape from thy sight,
> Keep them within thy heart.
> 22 For they are life to those who possess them,
> And health for all their flesh.[5]
>
> 23 More than all that needs to be guarded[6] control thy heart,
> For from it flow the springs of life.

---

[1] I have followed the majority of commentators in transposing vv. 18 and 19 to avoid two abrupt changes of subject.
[2] For this translation see G. R. Driver, *JTS* 35, 1934, p. 381.
[3] LXX '*my* instruction' (*mūsārī*) does not solve this problem, though if correct it would indicate that the verse originally referred to the instruction of the teacher.
[4] Other examples of relatively original discourses whose limits are defined by the nature of the following material are 1.8–19; 3.1–10; 4.20–27.
[5] Reading, following Gemser, *beśārām* for *beśārō* for reasons of grammar.
[6] For this interpretation of *mišmōr* see G.-K. 85 e-m. Cf. *The Words of Aḥiqar*, line 98 (A. Cowley, *Aramaic Papyri of the Fifth Century B.C.*, Oxford, 1923, p. 215).

The Book of the Ten Discourses

24 Put away from thee deceitful speech,
   And put crooked lips far from thee.
25 Let thine eyes look straight ahead,
   And thy glance be directed straight before thee.
27 Turn neither to the right nor to the left;
   Remove thy foot from evil.[1]
26 Examine[2] the path which thy feet tread,
   And all thy ways will be made sure.[3]

Discourse VIII. Avoidance of the 'Strange Woman'

5.1 My son, be attentive to my wisdom;
    To my perspicacity incline thine ear.
  2 Let discretion watch over thee,
    And let knowledge guard thy lips.[4]

   (Keeping thee from the 'strange woman',
    From the 'stranger' with her smooth words.)[5]
  3 For the lips of the 'stranger' drip honey,
    And smoother than oil is her speech;
  4 But her end is as bitter as wormwood,
    Sharp as a two-edged sword.
  5 Her feet go down towards death,
    To Sheol do her steps lead straight;
  6 So that[6] she seeks not out the path of life,
    Her ways are unsteady, she has no stability.[7]
  8 Take the road which is far from her,
    And go not near to the door of her house;[8]

---

[1] Transposition of vv. 26 and 27 gives a better sequence of thought and provides a stronger, positive conclusion to the discourse.

[2] For this translation of *pallēs* see G. R. Driver, *JTS* 36, 1935, pp. 150f., and D. Winton Thomas, *JTS* 37, 1936, p. 59.

[3] LXX here adds two extra verses, but these are universally agreed to be secondary.

[4] This tentative rendering is based on a conjectural emendation of a notoriously corrupt verse, unsatisfactory metrically, grammatically and in meaning. Various solutions have been offered, but none is completely satisfactory.

[5] Following a suggestion of Toy that a verse identical with 2.16 and 7.5 has accidentally dropped out. Without it the change of subject is too abrupt. All the 'strange woman' discourses then follow the same general pattern.

[6] See D. Winton Thomas, *JTS* 37, 1936, pp. 59f., for the unusual translation of *pen-*. An alternative would be a conjectural emendation to *bal-* or *lō'-*.

[7] Thomas (*ibid.*) distinguishes a verb *yādaʿ* 'be calm' (cognate with Arabic *waduʿa*) from the more common *yādaʿ* 'know' (cognate with Accadian *idū*).

[8] V. 7 interrupts the thought of the passage and has found its way into the text through some accident of copying, or by the inclusion of a gloss intended to emphasize the importance of the following words. Cf. 7.24.

21 For the ways of man are fully observed by Yahweh,
   And all his paths does he examine.¹

As in the case of Discourse IV, it is difficult to be sure where this discourse ends. There is no dramatic conclusion similar to that of Discourse II (2.18f.): the dreadful fate of those who associate with the strange woman has already been implied in v. 5. Verse 8 would make rather an abrupt ending, and of the verses which follow (9–23) v. 21 is perhaps most likely to have been the original conclusion. The remainder of these verses, in spite of a general similarity of theme, differ markedly from vv. 3–8 in style, vocabulary and point of view and also lack internal unity.² The strange woman is no longer mentioned (except for a brief reference in v. 20); the reason given for avoiding adultery in vv. 9–14 is quite different from that given in the other discourses about the strange woman; the mention of the congregation and assembly (v. 14) strikes a specifically Israelite note altogether foreign to the character of these instructions; the exhortation to marital fidelity (vv. 15–20) is inappropriate to instruction given to the young wisdom pupils; and the general statements about the fate of the wicked and the fool merely repeat what has already been said with greater force in v. 5. The discourse has been turned into a repository for heterogeneous sayings, mainly about chastity. (6.1–19, as is generally recognized, are an entirely secondary section.) Although the unity of the chapter has been questioned by some commentators, the secondary character of the latter part only becomes fully obvious when the first is seen as one of a series of short, compact and well-constructed discourses of the same type.

Discourse IX. Avoidance of the 'Strange Woman'

6.20 Keep, my son, the commandment of thy father,
   And reject not the teaching of thy mother.
21 Bind them constantly on thy heart,
   Tie them round thy neck.
22 When thou walkest, they will lead thee;
   When thou liest down they will watch over thee,³

¹ See p. 47, n. 2 *supra*.
² Cf. H. Renard, *Le Livre des Proverbes* (SB), 1951, *ad loc.*
³ This conjectural emendation has been obtained by omitting the third stichos and altering the two fem. sing. verbs to plurals, on the analogy of 3.24 and 4.12. On the difficulties of the verse see the commentaries.

The Book of the Ten Discourses

24 Keeping thee from the 'strange woman',[1]
   From the smooth tongue of the 'stranger'.
25 Desire not her beauty in thy heart,
   And let her not captivate thee with her glances.
32 He who commits adultery is without intelligence;
   A destroyer of his own life is he who does so.

Here, as in Discourse VIII, a quantity of secondary material concerning the folly of unchastity has been added to the original discourse. The direct address to the pupil ends with v. 25 and is succeeded by a series of general statements. In v. 26 the woman is no longer called *'iššā zārā* and *nokriyyā*, as regularly in the discourses, but *'iššā zōnā*, 'prostitute', and *'ēšet 'iš*, words never used in the discourses. Once again various practical reasons are given for chastity, in contrast to the simple statement of the discourses that the penalty for unchastity is death (v. 32, cf. 2.18f.; 5.5; 7.26f.). The rhetorical question (vv. 27, 28) is a form which does not occur elsewhere in the discourses. Verses 33–35 are an anticlimax after v. 32.

Verse 23 is an addition of a different kind. 23a is a gloss on v. 20, explaining the meaning of the words *miṣwā*, 'commandment', and *tōrā*, 'teaching', in terms of later orthodox Jewish wisdom in which 'lamp' and 'light' are synonymous with the word of Yahweh (Ps. 119.105). The second half of the verse is an unattached and unexplained observation similar to Prov. 10.17.

As with Discourse VIII, the striking difference between the simplicity and compactness of the original discourse and the diffuseness of the additional material has not been observed by the commentaries.

Discourse X. Avoidance of the 'Strange Woman'

7.1 My son, keep my words,
    And lay up my commandments with thee.
  2 Keep my commandments, and thou shalt live,
    And my teaching, as if it were the pupil of thine eye;
  3 Bind them on thy fingers,
    Write them on the tablet of thy heart.

---

[1] Reading *'iššā zārā* for *'ēšet rāʿ* on the analogy of 2.16 and 5.20 (Toy). This is preferable to the otherwise unknown 'woman of evil'; but see the commentaries for other possibilities.

Wisdom in Proverbs

5 That they may keep thee from the 'strange woman',
  From the 'stranger' with her smooth words.
25 Let not thy heart stray to her ways,
  Wander not into her paths:
26 For many a victim has she laid low,
  And those whom she has slain make a great host.
27 Her house is the way to Sheol,
  Leading down to the chambers of death.

This discourse has been greatly expanded by the addition of vv. 6–23, which (apart from the connecting word *kī*, 'for', at the beginning of v. 6) was originally a separate poem on a similar theme. Its omission (together with v. 24, which was probably inserted for the same reason as 5.7, and v. 4, which was added, like similar interpolations in other discourses, to the introduction to identify the words of the teacher with wisdom) reduces the discourse to the same length and form as the other discourses on this theme (II, VIII and IX). Verse 25 follows naturally on v. 5,[1] and the literary awkwardness of the double climax (vv. 23 and 27) is removed.

Verses 6–23 have their own internal problems,[2] but otherwise form a self-contained literary unit with its own introduction and conclusion. They are a vivid and polished moral story of a literary type quite distinct from that to which the discourses belong, which depends for its effect on the vividness of its descriptions and which describes in detail features which are only mentioned tersely in the discourses: the appearance of the woman, the wiles with which she seduces the young man.[3] Features which are entirely lacking in the discourses play a prominent part here: the sacrificial feast, the absence of the husband, the actual words of the woman. The narrative form describing a scene observed by the narrator[4] is also unique.

[1] Note that 6.24, 25 in Discourse IX provide a complete parallel. The two discourses, when the secondary material has been removed, are strikingly similar.
[2] Especially the corrupt state of vv. 22f. and the possibility that vv. 11f. may be an interpolation.
[3] The character of vv. 6–23 as a distinct unit does not appear to have been noticed by the commentators.
[4] There is no reason, in spite of theories about the cultic significance of this passage (on which see G. Boström, *Proverbiastudien: Die Weisheit und das fremde Weib in Spr.* 1–9, Lund, 1935, esp. pp. 104–55), to prefer the LXX text of vv. 6f., where it is the woman and not the narrator who looks out of the window.

The Book of the Ten Discourses

The subjects with which these ten discourses deal—avoidance of evil company, avoidance of entanglement with immoral women, duties towards God and neighbour, prudence and self-control—are subjects which one might find in any book of ethical teaching addressed to young men, and general parallels can be found for almost all of them in the Old Testament (not only in the wisdom books but in the prophets and the laws) and in Egyptian and Mesopotamian wisdom books.[1] Apart from general similarities of vocabulary between them and the Old Testament, which are due merely to the fact of a common language, however, it is not possible to point with certainty to a single case of direct literary dependence upon any extant text, either biblical or non-biblical.[2] However, as might be expected in the case of discourses whose introductory formulae and general preface show marked similarities to non-Israelite instructions of wisdom, the style and literary form are closer to those models than to the ethical passages of the Old Testament.[3] Unlike the sermons of Deuteronomy and the teaching of the prophets, this 'Book of the Ten Discourses' is a handbook of instruction designed for use in school and is addressed not to a whole community on the basis of a religious tradition but to individual pupils who are being prepared for adult life. In spite of some obvious differences, it is difficult to avoid a comparison with the Egyptian instructions, of which *Amen-em-opet* is the most outstanding example. Both are divided into fairly short chapters of

---

[1] For the former, see Robert, *art. cit.*, RB 43–44; for the latter, Humbert, *Recherches*.

[2] Probably the closest parallels are those concerned with avoidance of immoral women: compare Discourses II, VIII, IX, X with *Anii* (Erman, pp. 236, 240), *Ptahhotep* 18 (Erman, p. 60) and the Babylonian *Counsels of Wisdom* (Lambert, p. 103, lines 73–79); and the house which 'sinks down to death' (2.18; 7.27) from which there is no return (2.19) with the 'land of no return' in the *Descent of Ishtar to the Nether World* (*ANET*, pp. 106–9). But these are no more than general reminiscences of well-known themes.

[3] The most important parallels of theme, apart from those already mentioned, are: Avoidance of evil company (Discourses, I, VI): *Anii* (Erman, pp. 237, 240), *Amen-em-opet* IX, 11.13f.; 13.8f.; reverence toward God (Discourse III): *Merikerē* (Erman, pp. 78f.; 83), *Anii* (Erman, pp. 235, 236, 239); relations with neighbours (Discourse IV): *Amen-em-opet, passim*; vigilance and prudence (Discourse VII): *Aḥiqar*, line 98 (Cowley, p. 215), *Counsels of Wisdom*, lines 26f. (Lambert, p. 101), *Ptahhotep*, epilogue (Erman, p. 63). This by no means exhausts the list. See further in Humbert, *Recherches*.

roughly equal length; both have prefaces which set out the purpose and virtues of the book in virtually the same terms.

Yet the book, in spite of its dependence on a foreign wisdom tradition, is in Israelite dress. Unlike Prov. 31.1–9, whose title frankly admits that it is an instruction given to a foreign king by his mother, it claims to be the 'proverbs of Solomon the son of David, king of Israel' (1.1). When it has occasion to mention the name of God it uses the name 'Yahweh'. Unlike the Egyptian instructions, it is not addressed to the young men of a particular class, but to all who are prepared to pay heed.[1] This characteristic reflects the comparatively unstratified character of Israelite society in contrast with that of Egypt. A further specifically Israelite characteristic is the use of certain words—especially, in the preface and introductory formulae, a variety of synonyms for wisdom and instruction—which are not simply translations of foreign terms but must belong to a specifically Israelite context.

In the course of the analysis of these chapters it has been suggested that some of the secondary material was added in order to modify the teaching of the discourses by equating the words of the wisdom teacher with an objectified or personified wisdom of which there is no mention in the discourses themselves, or to attribute the salutary effects of obeying them to Yahweh. It is therefore necessary to examine the fundamental concepts of the discourses in order to determine more closely the reason for these additions. Their literary form, vocabulary and themes show signs of both foreign and Israelite influence; but only an examination of their fundamental ideas can show their true character.

---

[1] On Egyptian wisdom as a class ethic see Gemser and Gese (*op. cit.*). But Brunner, *Erziehung*, pp. 40–42, claims that Egyptian education was, at least in some periods, not absolutely confined to one class; and on the Israelite side it is improbable that the children of poor parents were usually able to take advantage of the education offered by the Israelite wisdom schools. However, the fact remains that most of the Egyptian discourses state specifically that their teaching is offered only to the scribal class, while these discourses do not.

III

THE TEN DISCOURSES AND THE EGYPTIAN INSTRUCTIONS: FUNDAMENTAL CONCEPTS

A. THE EGYPTIAN INSTRUCTIONS

THE type of literary composition whose ideas are here compared with those of the discourses is that which has been defined by Brunner[1] as follows: 'the literary type of those works which contain an instruction of a teacher to a pupil (often in the form of an instruction of a father to his son) or the fiction of such an instruction. The teacher guides his pupil to a right attitude towards life on the basis of his own experience, and above all on the basis of knowledge which has been transmitted to him.' We may thus begin by noting that the ten discourses correspond absolutely to this definition, which might well have been written about them.

Brunner lists seven such instructions as surviving in a more or less complete form, but we now possess eight, which may be arranged with some confidence in chronological order thus:

The Instruction of Ptahhotep (Old Kingdom, perhaps *c.* 2400 BC)
The Instruction for King Merikerē (10th dynasty, *c.* 2100 BC)
The Instruction of King Amenemhēt (12th dynasty, *c.* 1960 BC)
The Instruction of Cheti the son of Duauf (perhaps 12th dynasty)
The Wisdom of Anii (18th dynasty, perhaps *c.* 1200 BC)
The Instruction of Amen-em-opet (22nd to 26th dynasties, *c.* 1000–600 BC)
Papyrus Insinger (an anonymous demotic instruction) (Persian or Greek period)
The Instruction of ʿOnchsheshonqy (perhaps 5th or 4th century).[2]

[1] *Handbuch*, p. 90.
[2] Translations of *Cheti* in Erman, pp. 67–72, and *ANET*, pp. 432–4; of ʿOnchsheshonqy in S. R. K. Glanville, *The Instructions of ʿOnchsheshonqy (Catalogue of Demotic Papyri in the British Museum* II), London, 1955. See also B. Gemser, 'The Instructions of ʿOnchsheshonqy and Biblical Wisdom Literature', *Congress Volume, Oxford 1959* (VT Suppl. 7), Leiden 1960, pp. 102–28.

Since we possess fragments of instructions even older than *Ptahhotep*, which is clearly far from being a first attempt at this kind of composition, we may say that the Egyptian instruction is a literary form which flourished for well over 2,000 years, during the course of which Israelite wisdom literature came into existence and passed through its first stages. In view of its very long history, it is remarkable how little the Egyptian instruction changed either in form, contents or general point of view.[1] Although the various works naturally reflect to some extent the changing social conditions and moods of the times in which they were written—especially the change from serene untroubled confidence in the Old Kingdom to a more sombre, troubled mood in the Middle Kingdom, and again to an increased trust in a gracious god in the later New Kingdom, in which ethical and religious motives, previously implicit, were now expressed more explicitly—a single, distinct, definite attitude to life can nevertheless be discerned in all of them. Its persistence through so long a period was due partly to the fact that in spite of all its social and political vicissitudes Egyptian society succeeded to a remarkable extent in returning to the old ways after each upheaval and never completely lost confidence in them, and partly to the limited aim of the instructions, which was primarily not to comment philosophically on contemporary problems, but rather to provide a practical education which would enable the pupils to deal successfully with whatever problems life set them. They are based on a confidence that the well-tried methods of past generations are still the best, and do not seek to devise new ones.

1. *The concept of Maat* Although the teaching of the instructions was fundamentally pragmatic, it was far from being merely opportunistic. Such an attitude would have been utterly condemned by their authors. On the contrary, it is conformity to the established customs of society which is constantly stressed, and

[1] Against the earlier evolutionary views of J. H. Breasted (*Development of Thought and Religion in Ancient Egypt*, London, 1912; *The Dawn of Conscience*, New York, 1934), more recent Egyptologists (de Buck, *art. cit.*, NTT 21; Frankfort, *Ancient Egyptian Religion*, pp. 54–82; Brunner, *Erziehung, passim* and *Handbuch*, pp. 90–110) have demonstrated the basic continuity of thought of the Egyptian instructions. This had already been appreciated to some extent by R. Anthes, *Lebensregeln und Lebensweisheit der alten Ägypter* (Das Alte Orient 32, Heft 2), Leipzig, 1933.

The Ten Discourses and the Egyptian Instructions

those customs themselves were not made by men for their convenience but belonged to a divinely established order of things. This order was reverenced as embracing all that was right and true, and was never very far from the thoughts of those who directed the education of youth. Thus in the instructions even 'statements which have for us a pragmatic ring appear to be transfused with a religious reverence'.[1] But this is a reverence not primarily for the gods or for any one particular god, but for the order itself: to 'the true divine Order, which extends equally over the Cosmos and the world of men, and which directly determines the conceptual unity of both'.[2] Here the instructions are in complete conformity with Egyptian thought in general. The name which the Egyptians gave to this divine order was *maat*. *Maat* was worshipped as a goddess, but this is not its primary meaning. Like wisdom in Israel, *maat* underwent a process of hypostatization which resulted, in polytheistic Egypt, in its being reckoned as a goddess; but primarily it was an abstract noun and was so used commonly in Egypt without any personal reference. It is such an all-embracing concept that its translation has often proved difficult. In some passages it approximates to 'justice' or 'right'; in others to 'truth'. Thus one speaks *maat*, does *maat* and follows *maat*. It is clearly distinguishable from the gods, in that not only does the king 'live' by *maat*, but so also do the gods.[3] It was given to men in remote antiquity as the basis of society.

It is in this sense that the instructions use the word. The fullest description of it is found in *Ptahhotep*, where it is said of it that

> It is good and its worth lasting, and it hath not been disturbed since the day of its creator, whereas he who transgresses its ordinances is punished. It lieth as a (right) path in front of him that knoweth nothing. Wrong-doing hath never yet brought its venture to port. Evil indeed winneth wealth, but the strength of truth (*maat*) is that it endureth, and the (upright) man saith: 'It is the property of my father.'[4]

---

[1] Frankfort, *op. cit.*, p. 65. Cf. Brunner, *Erziehung*, pp. 2f., and Gese, *Lehre und Wirklichkeit*, pp. 7–11. These three works together with Brunner's 'Weisheitsliteratur' in the *Handbuch der Orientalistik* (*loc. cit.*) contain the most reliable accounts of the basic concepts of Egyptian wisdom literature and Egyptian thought generally.
[2] Brunner, *Erziehung*, p. 118. Cf. Frankfort, pp. 54–56; Gese, pp. 12ff.
[3] Frankfort, *op. cit.*, pp. 54f.
[4] *Ptahhotep* 5 (Erman, p. 57). Compare the translation in *ANET*, p. 412, where *maat* is translated by 'justice' rather than 'truth' as in Erman.

Admonitions to 'do' and to 'speak' *maat* are found in the instructions of all later periods, down to the late ʿ*Onchsheshonqy*.[1]

The doing of *maat* is the key to a long and prosperous life:

> I have spent 110 years in life, which the king has given me, and with rewards beyond those of them that have gone before, because I did right (*maat*) for the king.[2]

It is not, however, something revealed supernaturally to each individual, but through the 'sayings of the ancestors' handed down to each generation by the instructors.[3]

2. *The gods* The gods do not go entirely unmentioned in the instructions, but the rather distinctive way in which they are mentioned indicates that their role, though it should not be underestimated, was regarded as taking second place to that of *maat*. Although Egypt possessed a pantheon and a rich mythology, the gods are here usually not mentioned by name, and the mythology is almost never referred to.[4] Indeed, the instructions do not refer to 'the gods', but simply, in the singular, to 'God' or 'the god'.[5] There has been much discussion whether this usage indicates that the authors of the instructions were monotheists, or at least that their thought tended towards monotheism, but such a view is improbable. It would involve the further conclusion that there were in Egypt virtually two religions, at least from the time of *Merikerē* at the beginning of the second millennium.[6] Nevertheless this usage strongly suggests that the authors of the instructions recognized that there was a fundamental unity in the divine

---

[1] E.g. *Merikerē* (Erman, p. 76); *Amen-em-opet* XIX, 20.14f.; XX, 21.5f.; ʿ*Onchsheshonqy* 13.15.

[2] *Ptahhotep* (Erman, p. 65).

[3] *Merikerē* (Erman, p. 76).

[4] Apart from *Amen-em-opet* the only clear mythological allusion is in a passage in *Merikerē* (Erman, p. 83; *ANET*, p. 417) in which 'God' (unnamed) is said to be the creator of heaven and earth and the protector of men. There may also be allusions here to a primeval battle, but the reference is a general one, and the point seems to be that man can rely on the divine providence.

[5] Since the king of Egypt is also regularly referred to as 'the god', it is important not to confuse these two meanings. But in most cases it is clear what the meaning is from the context.

[6] Possibly even from the time of *Ptahhotep*, although it is possible that the references to 'god' there refer to the king.

The Ten Discourses and the Egyptian Instructions

purpose.¹ Such a view would, indeed, seem to be a necessary corollary of the belief in *maat* as the divine order.

At first sight *Amen-em-opet*, which has been shown to be similar in other ways to the discourses in Prov. 1-9, seems to be an exception to this way of thinking. The author, while he does not abandon the language of his predecessors, and indeed speaks of 'God' or 'the universal Lord' in more than half of his references to divinity, nevertheless refers also to a number of other Egyptian gods: *Thoth*, *Khnūm*, *Aten*, *Rē*, and *Shay* and *Renenut* (the deified concepts of 'fate' and 'fortune'). Sometimes the particular characteristics of these deities are mentioned: e.g. *Khnūm* as the potter who fashions men on his wheel (IX, 12.15f.). The reason for the unparalleled use of the divine names in this instruction is not clear;² but the very fact that the author uses both kinds of terminology indifferently shows that, although he gives greater prominence to the individual gods than his predecessors, he has by no means abandoned their belief in a single, all-embracing order. *Maat* is now quite definitely associated with 'God':

Maat is a great gift of God;
He will give it to whom he will.

(XX, 21.5f.)

The functions of the other gods, even though they are mentioned in connexion with the features traditionally associated with them, are not really distinct from one another, but are simply aspects of the function of 'God' as universal Lord and judge of men. Thus sometimes it is *Thoth* who judges and rewards men (XVI, 18.2f.; and as the Moon, II, 4.19; VI, 7.19, or the Ape, XV, 17.9-12; XVI, 17.22-18.1), but elsewhere it is the Eye of *Rē* (XVII, 18.23-19.1); but it is *Aten* in whose hands man's good fortune lies (VII,

---

¹ See especially H. Stock, 'Ägyptische Religionsgeschichte', *Saeculum* 1, 1950, pp. 613-36. His conclusion is that the 'God' of the Egyptian wisdom literature is neither a sole god distinct from the pantheon, nor a member of the pantheon, but 'everything related to the numinous' (p. 635).

² Brunner, *Handbuch*, p. 108, believes that it is due to the unsettled times in which the instruction was written. The partial breakdown of the social order had led to a diminished confidence in *maat* as something which could be taken for granted. Since it was no longer so obviously visible, men had to be exhorted to find their norm of conduct in *maat* as expressed in the will of the individual gods. But Brunner stresses that the belief in *maat* as the gift of God is no less strong here than in the earlier instructions.

Wisdom in Proverbs

10.12–15), and *Khnūm* whose function is to 'mould and burn hearts' (IX, 12.15f.). These functions are clearly not intended to be distinct from one another, and similar functions are attributed to 'God' or the 'universal Lord' in other passages. This fluidity of thought is, according to Frankfort, typical of Egyptian religion. The Egyptian gods never became complete, fully-formed concepts possessing true independence, but remained 'captive within their own manifestations'.[1] Egyptian religion is thus, although not a monotheism, nevertheless only an incomplete polytheism. Thus, even though it may be said that *maat* is a divine gift to men, 'the gods live by *maat*', and are not independent of it. There is no fundamental difference between the teaching of *Amen-em-opet* and the earlier instructions.

In all the instructions from *Ptahhotep* to *Amen-em-opet* (and in the later ones also) the function of God in relation to man is practically restricted to that of maintainer of the world order, judge and dispenser of the due rewards which fall to man in accordance with their conformity or non-conformity to *maat*. God sees and knows all that man does;[2] he loves righteous men and their deeds and abominates unrighteousness;[3] he gives prosperity or brings men to ruin as they deserve.[4] Only occasionally do we find the idea that God's ways are mysterious and his judgments inscrutable.[5] In general the instructions reflect confidence in the divine providence.

The above account of the doctrine of God in the Egyptian instructions may have given the impression that God plays a more important part there than is actually the case. In fact, the references to God are comparatively few, and the statements about the inevitability of retribution in which God is not mentioned are far more numerous than those where he is. This is true even of *Amen-em-opet*, where, for example, there is no mention of God at all in the opening chapter where the author claims that attention to his teaching is in itself entirely sufficient to ensure prosperity.

---

[1] *Op. cit.*, pp. 25–28.
[2] *Merikerē* (Erman, pp. 77, 79, 83); *Amen-em-opet, passim*.
[3] *Ptahhotep* 12, 22, 30 and epilogue (Erman, pp. 59, 61f., 64); *Amen-em-opet* X, 13.15f.; 14.2; XIII, 15.21.
[4] *Ptahhotep* 22, 30 (Erman, pp. 61, 62); *Merikerē* (Erman, p. 77); *Anii* (Erman, pp. 238, 239); *Amen-em-opet, passim*.
[5] *Amen-em-opet* XVIII, 19.13–17; XXI, 22.5f.

The Ten Discourses and the Egyptian Instructions

There is little or no suggestion of the possibility of a personal relationship between man and God. Direct duties toward God, which consist of the due performance of cultic obligations, are treated in the same way as other admonitions, as items in a list of rules whose neglect will entail serious consequences.[1] The idea that a man should perform such duties for any motive other than his own safety and prosperity is lacking.[2]

3. *The ideal man* The character of the ideal man can be summarized by saying that he conforms in every respect to *maat*. The ideal changed very little, except to some extent in the way in which it was expressed, throughout Egyptian history, but it is in *Amen-em-opet* that we find it most fully expressed. One whole chapter (IV) is devoted to the contrast between the characters and fates of the ideal man and his opposite, but the thought of these two types of conduct permeates the whole work. The ideal man is called the 'truly silent' or 'tranquil' man (*gr m'*) and is contrasted with the 'hot' or 'passionate' man (*šmm*). 'Silence' as an ideal first appears in *Ptahhotep*.[3] It is to be interpreted both literally and symbolically. Success and security in Egyptian life depended to a great extent on the judicious use of speech: what to say in different circumstances, how to express it, and when to keep silent. To speak injudiciously would be to invite at the least contempt, and at the worst punishment. So one should always 'pause before speaking' (*Amen-em-opet* II, 5.7f.) and avoid quarrels and disputes (III, 5.10f.) and indiscreet revelations of one's private thoughts (XXI, 22.11–14). But the concept of 'silence' went deeper than this. Speech was the revelation of character. Too much talking was the sign of a lack of self-control, and for this reason the 'silent man' was considered to be a superior person, the opposite not only of the 'talker' but of the 'passionate' or 'uncontrolled' person whose lack of self-control extended into other spheres of action besides speech. 'Silence' or 'tranquillity' was not a *negative* characteristic revealing weakness of character, but on the contrary

---

[1] *Merikerē* (Erman, pp. 78f., 82f.); *Anii* (Erman, pp. 235, 239). Cf. *Amen-em-opet* VII, 10,12–15.

[2] The remarkably 'scriptural' statement, 'More acceptable (to God) is the virtue of one that is just of heart than the ox of him that does iniquity' (*Merikerē*, Erman, p. 83), is no exception, as the context shows.

[3] *Ptahhotep* 1–4, 24 (Erman, pp. 56, 61).

Wisdom in Proverbs

a token of a *positive* attitude to life based on an understanding of, and a confidence in, the Order. A man who has been injured is counselled not to seek revenge, not because he may get the worst of it a second time, but because there is no need to do so:

> Sit thee down at the hands of God;
> Thy tranquillity will overthrow them.
> (XXI, 22.7f.)

The meaning of this 'overthrowing' is made clear in chapter IV: the 'passionate' man, though success may come to him at first, will come suddenly to a bad end (IV, 6.1–6), while the 'truly silent' man will go from strength to strength (IV, 6.7–12). The concept of the 'silent man' is thus based on a confidence in the operation of *maat*, the Order which can be relied upon; and the character of the 'silent man', in spite of the use of a term which seems to be negative, is a positive one based on that confidence, accepting and enjoying all that is good in life without a trace of asceticism or self-denial.[1]

This ideal had remained virtually unchanged since early times. The importance of the proper use of speech (as well as the positive value of silence) is stressed in the Old Kingdom *Ptahhotep*, the Middle Kingdom *Merikerē*[2] and the New Kingdom *Anii*[3] as well as in *Amen-em-opet*. Already in *Ptahhotep* self-control is the principle which underlies warnings against intellectual pride, greed, entanglement with women and covetousness;[4] and the purpose of this self-control is practical rather than ascetical, as the section recommending the pupil to 'follow his heart' seems to indicate.[5] The device of drawing a contrast between the ideal man and his opposite also goes back to *Ptahhotep*, who contrasts the man who 'hearkens' with the man who does not,[6] expressions which were still in use in the time of *Amen-em-opet*. The three rules of hearkening (to teachers and superiors), silence and caution in speaking all express fundamentally the same ideal: respect for and conformity

---

[1] E.g. I, 3.17f.; V, 7.10; XIII, 16.13f.; XX, 21.17f. On this point see Anthes, *op. cit.*, p. 31; Brunner, *Erziehung*, p. 123.
[2] Erman, pp. 75f.
[3] Erman, pp. 235, 236, 238, 240.
[4] *Ptahhotep* 1, 7, 18, 19, 20 (Erman, pp. 56, 57, 60, 61).
[5] *Ibid.*, 11 (Erman, pp. 58f.)
[6] Prologue (p. 55) and Epilogue (pp. 63f.).

The Ten Discourses and the Egyptian Instructions

to the established order of society. The only real folly is to rebel against them in order to follow one's own whims and passions. The one course leads to success and happiness, the other to disaster.

4. *The nature of authority and the purpose of the instructions* These matters have already been mentioned.[1] Although they teach that man is dependent on the will of the gods, the authors of the instructions make no claim to reveal that will to their pupils. Their authority is entirely human. They do not even make a personal claim to the exclusive possession of wisdom. Their teaching is available to any intelligent person, since it is nothing more than the wisdom of an ordinary mature person, compounded from the traditional teaching which they have received and their own experience of life. This knowledge of the world is thus knowledge (within the limits of human possibility) of the nature of *maat*, and it is this which constitutes both the authority of the teacher and the content of his teaching. Thus the good life is something which can be taught, communicated by one man to another without any need for divine revelation. It is basically no more than common sense. But such was the strength of tradition in Egypt that we hear nothing of conflicting schools of teaching; and the instructions of all periods differ remarkably little from one another, either in contents or in general point of view. The claim made by the author of *Amen-em-opet* that his instruction sets the pupil 'on the path of life' (prologue, 1.7) and ensures success (I, 3.17f.) may be taken as summing up the purpose of all of them. But the teacher possesses no coercive power—he can only say that his teaching is in conformity to *maat*, to the will of the gods, and to the teaching of the ancestors, and point out as vividly as possible the respective consequences of following, and ignoring, his advice.

B. THE TEN DISCOURSES

1. *The concept of Order* There is no equivalent in Hebrew for the Egyptian word *maat*. The word *ḥokmā*, which otherwise plays such a prominent part in Old Testament wisdom literature,[2]

---

[1] See pp. 35-37, *supra*.
[2] Of the 350 occurrences of the words 'wise', 'wisdom' and their cognates, over half are in Proverbs, Job and Ecclesiastes.

Wisdom in Proverbs

occurs only three times in the discourses,[1] and there it has no particular significance, but is merely one of a number of synonyms which stress the value of the teaching given by the wisdom instructor.[2] Words like *ṣedeq* (righteousness), *mišpāṭ* (justice) and *mēšārīm* (right conduct) which occur together in 1.3; 2.9 approach *maat* in one of its meanings, but the very wealth of synonyms shows that there is no real equivalent. *mūsār* (instruction, 1.2, 3, 8; 4.1) corresponds rather to the Egyptian *seboyet* and refers either to the contents or method of the instruction given in the school.

Yet although the author of the discourses[3] apparently did not attempt to find a single term to render the Egyptian *maat*, there underlies the discourses a concept of a fundamental universal order which is quite different from the normal teaching of the Old Testament,[4] but remarkably similar to the Egyptian concept. While it is true that in three passages (3.5–10, 32; 5.21) man's happiness is said to be derived from divine favour, more frequently we find a concept of a just retribution which is expressed simply as a universal law, with no specific reference to the will of God (1.18f.; 2.19; 4.18f.; 5.3–6; 6.32, etc.). Even in those passages where the will of God is mentioned, some of the expressions used suggest Egyptian rather than Yahwistic influence, especially 'abomination to Yahweh' (3.32) and 'the ways of man are before the eyes of Yahweh' (5.21), two phrases which were particular favourites (*mutatis mutandis*) with the author of *Amen-em-opet*.

It is this universal law which the wisdom teacher, who has himself received it from human sources, seeks to impart to his pupil. In the greatest possible contrast to the teaching of the Old Testament, but in perfect conformity with Egyptian teaching, it

---

[1] 1.2; 4.11; 5.1. The word 'wise' (*ḥākām*) occurs once (3.7).

[2] The words 'wise', 'wisdom', which were also known to the Canaanites (the god *El* is called wise in the Ugaritic texts) were common words in Hebrew from early times (Judg. 5.29). Wisdom did not necessarily connote a divine quality or gift (for its use in a bad sense see II Sam. 13.3) and was therefore suitable for use in this way by a teacher who did not claim inspiration.

[3] In the following pages the word 'discourses' will be used to designate the Ten Discourses of Prov. 1–9, and the word 'instructions' to designate the Egyptian instructions.

[4] This concept, like some of the other fundamental concepts of the discourses, is also found in some other O.T. wisdom passages. See Würthwein, *Die Weisheit Ägyptens*, p. 5, and Gese, *op. cit.*, pp. 33–38. The purpose of the present study is restricted to a comparison of the thought of the discourses with that of the instructions.

The Ten Discourses and the Egyptian Instructions

is taken for granted that there is no conflict between the desires and ambitions of man and the demands of God.[1]

In general the existence of this law is taken for granted without need for detailed description. Certain actions lead to happiness; others to destruction. It is, however, sometimes expressed by the metaphor of walking along a road—a metaphor which, since it is used frequently both in Egyptian teaching and in the Old Testament, is probably very ancient. A man's fate is determined by where he walks (1.15; 5.21) and how he walks (4.25f.). Fools and sinners walk on the path which leads to destruction (1.15–18; 2.18f.; 4.14f., 19; 5.5, 6, 8; 7.25); but there is a way which leads to happiness and prosperity: the way which follows the teacher's advice (3.23; 4.11f., 18, 26). This is a straight way, turning neither to the right nor to the left (4.25–27) and is to be carefully examined to ensure that it is the right one (4.26; 5.21). To walk along it is like walking in the bright sunlight (4.18). In most cases this way, the choice of which is decisive for every individual, is not specifically associated with God, but is to be found simply by following the instructions of the teacher who is a qualified guide (e.g. 4.10f.).

2. *Doctrine of God* The attitude of the author of the discourses toward God is more straightforward than that of his Egyptian counterpart. His task was less confusing: for him, as an Israelite, there was only one God who was relevant to his readers, and his name was Yahweh. Apart from two verses of no theological significance (2.17; 3.4), all the references to God in the discourses call him by his name Yahweh.[2]

Yet the role which God plays in the discourses is essentially the same as that of the gods and 'God' in the instructions, and quite different from his role in the rest of the Old Testament. The very fact of the infrequency of reference to him (only five: 3.5, 7, 9, 32; 5.21) is sufficient to indicate this. But more than this, almost every aspect of the Old Testament doctrine of God is lacking. Nothing is said of his righteousness, love, wrath, judgment, creation and preservation of the world, his covenant with Israel, the possibility of a personal relationship with him, or his

---

[1] See W. Zimmerli, 'Zur Struktur der alttestamentlichen Weisheit', *ZAW* 51, 1933, p. 203.
[2] There is no reason to prefer the LXX reading 'God' in 3.5, 7; 5.21.

mystery. He remains in the background, apparently impersonal and remote. It is also significant that of the five references to him, three are placed in a special section (Discourse III, 3.1–10) devoted to 'duties toward God'. This arrangement, which is reminiscent of *Merikerē*, has the effect of removing him almost completely from the rest of the discourses and making him simply one subject of the curriculum.

Only three functions are attributed to Yahweh in the discourses:

(*a*) *He may be relied on as a guide through life* (3.5f.) It is implied here and in the following verse that he possesses a higher wisdom than does man. Yet in other passages (e.g. 3.1f.; 4.10–12) the wisdom teacher claims no less for himself and his own human knowledge of the way the world works. This single acknowledgment of God's wisdom and providence hardly seems to represent the focal point of the teaching of the discourses.

(*b*) *He sees all, examines and judges human conduct* (5.21; 3.32) These statements are very close to the thought of *Amen-em-opet*, and completely lack the passion in which the judgment of God is expressed in the Old Testament. Nothing is said about the grounds on which God judges men, or of the capacity in which he does it. Elsewhere in the Old Testament he does so as the creator of the world, or as the God of the covenant, and on the basis of his own holiness or righteousness. But on these characteristics the discourses are silent. It is not suggested that he created the established order within whose framework he exercises his function of judge, or that he established the standards by which he judges, or that he teaches men his laws. It is the wisdom teacher who teaches what is the norm, who urges the pupil to conform to it, and who claims the right to command. Thus, although we cannot expect to find a complete description of the nature of God in so few verses, the impression which they give is that there is no independent will or action on God's part. He merely observes man's conduct and puts into operation the inflexible rules which govern the world.[1]

---

[1] On this see especially G. Bertram, 'Die religiöse Umdeutung altorientalischer Lebensweisheit in der griechischen Übersetzung des AT's', *ZAW* 54, 1936, p. 153; cf. Zimmerli, *art. cit.*, pp. 189–91, 203; Würthwein, *op. cit.*, pp. 9–11. It may be noted that in some religions—e.g. the Egyptian—the all-seeing god and the judge of men was not necessarily the same as the creator god.

The Ten Discourses and the Egyptian Instructions

(*c*) *He gives men the due reward for their conduct:* 'straight paths' (3.6); health (3.8); material prosperity (3.10). It is perhaps significant that even here in two out of three of these verses the giving of the reward is described impersonally or negatively: if a man fears Yahweh and departs from evil *'that will be* healing' for his flesh; if one honours Yahweh with one's wealth, one's barns *will be filled* with grain. It is not directly said that Yahweh will give healing or will fill the barns. The author appears to be anxious to avoid attributing even this degree of personal action to God. The performance of his duties to God is part of the proper behaviour of man; but the idea that the giving of rewards is part of the working of an impersonal order seems to prevail over the concept of a God who has a personal relationship with men and a personal will upon which men depend. The impression is given that this God, even though he is called 'Yahweh', is rather a functionary carrying out the requirements of an impersonal order than a God who himself decides man's fate.[1]

3. *The ideal man* Like the Egyptian instructions, the discourses describe two types of man: the ideal man and his opposite. Indeed, this seems to have been their primary aim. Unlike the much longer instructions they do not attempt to give detailed and comprehensive instruction covering every situation (this was no doubt given in other parts of the curriculum) but select certain themes through which the fundamental character of the ideal man is illustrated both positively and negatively. To some extent the same terminology is used as in the Egyptian instructions: the importance of 'hearing' is stressed (1.5, 8; 4.1, 10, 20; 5.1); the metaphor of the 'way of life' is frequently employed. On the other hand, the importance of 'silence' or 'tranquillity', which is stressed elsewhere in Proverbs (17.27f.; 21.23; 29.11, etc.) is not mentioned; and occasionally the two types are designated by characteristically Hebrew expressions: 'the wise man' (1.5) and the man who is 'devoid of intelligence' (6.32).

But apart from the terminology the characters of the two types are remarkably similar to their Egyptian counterparts. The ideal

---

[1] Zimmerli's comment that this is a God whose function is to do what man wants (*art. cit.*, p. 189) is, however, an exaggeration. Man's desires are only fulfilled in as far as they conform to the order.

man has two main characteristics, which are interrelated: conformity to the norm and self-control; his opposite is the man who rebels against the norm and surrenders himself to human passions.

(*a*) *Conformity to the norm* This characteristic is most clearly illustrated in Discourse VII on the importance of vigilance. The ideal man keeps to the middle way, the way of conformity to the prescribed social order, and refuses to turn aside from it (4.25-27). The same principle appears in the other discourses. The ideal man avoids the enemies of society, who seek to overthrow it by violence (I, 1.10-19; VI, 4.14-19),[1] and does not envy them (IV, 3.31). He refuses to be led astray into adultery—a practice equally disruptive of society (II, VIII, IX, X). He avoids intellectual pride, submitting himself to the superior wisdom of God (III, 3.5-8). He performs the prescribed religious duties (III, 3.9f.). He acknowledges the customary obligations of the man who has been blessed with material sufficiency by generosity to less fortunate neighbours (IV, 3.27f.). He lives at peace with his neighbours (IV, 3.29f.). He speaks the truth—another practice essential to the well-being of society (VII, 4.24).

In contrast the man whose conduct is to be avoided is a rebel against society, represented by the robbers and murderers who urge the young man to join them (I), the adulteress who has broken the marriage vow and 'forgotten the covenant of her god' (II, 2.17) and whose conduct leads straight to destruction, and by the various kinds of behaviour which the pupil is instructed to avoid: intellectual pride and neglect of religious duties (III); lack of responsibility towards others, trouble-making (IV); lying and deceit (VII, 4.24).

(*b*) *Self-control* In almost every discourse the need to resist temptation is emphasized. The basic requirement is vigilance: a special emphasis is placed on control over the heart (*lēb*, the seat of vital energy, inner man, disposition, will, intelligence),[2] which is said to be the 'source of the springs of life' (VII, 4.23) and corresponds in general to the 'heart' in the Egyptian instructions. Vigilance is

---

[1] In the following pages Roman numerals indicate the number of the discourse; Arabic numerals chapter and verse.

[2] L. Koehler and W. Baumgartner, *Lexicon in Veteris Testamenti Libros*, Brill, Leiden, 1953, *art. lēb*, pp. 469f.

The Ten Discourses and the Egyptian Instructions

thus to be exercised at the very centre of the human will. This total self-control, which strongly resembles the Egyptian 'silence', expresses itself in speaking the truth, in concentration on one's allotted task, and in keeping to the prescribed rules of behaviour (mouth, eyes, feet, VII, 4.24–27). The need for self-control is most vividly expressed in the four discourses about the temptations of the adulteress, a subject which is dealt with in somewhat the same way in the Egyptian instructions. It is the adulteress who above all lacks self-control: 'her ways are unsteady, she has no stability' (5.6). So she and her victim, who share the same weakness, also end by sharing the same fate.

Self-control thus enables a man to resist all temptations: the persuasive words of criminals when they urge him by promises of reward to join their gang (I, 1.10–15); the seductive words and glances of the adulteress (II, 2.16; VIII, 5.3; IX, 6.24f.; X, 7.5), and, by implication, the temptations to the deadly sins of greed (I), avarice (IV, 3.27f.), anger and cruelty (IV, 3.30f.; VI, 4.16–18). Again the picture of the ideal man is heightened by descriptions of the fate of those who lack this essential virtue of self-control (I, 1.19; VIII, 5.4–6; IX, 6.32).

The contrast between the fates of these two types of man is expressed in various ways, of which the most striking is the repeated contrast between 'life' and 'death'.

4. *The nature of authority and the purpose of the discourses* It is not possible to discern any difference on these two points between the instructions and the discourses. The author of the discourses, like his Egyptian counterpart, appeals to no authority other than his own. Words like *tōrā* (instruction), *dābār* (word) and *miṣwā* (commandment), which are used elsewhere in the Old Testament of God's commands, are here used exclusively of the teacher's. The authority of the teacher is said to be wholly reliable and thus, in one sense, absolute, yet in the nature of the case it is not authority in a coercive sense. The instruction was no doubt accompanied by corporal punishment,[1] but it could never be more than advice. The pupil must co-operate: he must be convinced that it is in his

---

[1] This is one of the meanings of *mūsār* ('instruction' or 'discipline'—cf. Prov. 13.24; 22.15; 23.13), as it is also one of the meanings of the corresponding Egyptian *seboyet*.

Wisdom in Proverbs

own interest to accept the teaching as his rule of life; and the real weapon in the hand of the teacher is persuasion. There is no mention of divine help: in the end it is the individual who must choose between the way of life and the way of death. This standpoint is very far removed from the Yahwistic point of view, according to which it is Yahweh who sets the alternatives of life and death before his people, and Yahweh who gives the strength to follow the path of life (Deut. 30.11–20).

The purpose of the discourses is, like that of the instructions, entirely concentrated on the well-being of the pupil, and the notion that the purpose of human life is to serve and glorify God is entirely absent. Their whole spirit is anthropocentric. There is no reference to God either in the preface or in any of the ten introductions. It is man who holds the centre of the stage: man not as God's creature but man seeking and receiving the answer to questions which relate solely to his own personal ambitions and desires. As Zimmerli remarked about Israelite wisdom literature in general, these questions can really be summed up in the one question: 'What is best for man?'—and the word 'best' ($\underline{t}\bar{o}b$), which is frequently used in the wisdom literature, has here no specific religious sense, but refers simply to man's desire for happiness.[1] At the same time, as in the Egyptian instructions, there is no anti-religious sentiment here. It is merely that, as in Egyptian wisdom literature, the principal subject is not God but man.

The teacher claims that the education which he gives is entirely sufficient to enable the pupil to achieve everything which is desirable in life: health, wealth, material success, happiness, longevity. The key word is 'life' ($hayyīm$), which according to its contexts means 'longevity' (2.19; 4.10), 'health' (4.22) and 'fullness of life' or 'joyful, prosperous life' (3.2; 5.6).[2] Other expressions are also employed: 'every path which leads to happiness ($\underline{t}\bar{o}b$)', 2.9; 'favour and a good reputation in the sight of God and man', 3.4. Security and stability are promised in 4.12, 18f.; 6.22; material wealth in 3.10. No distinction is made between material and spiritual gifts: in 2.9 happiness is identified with three moral virtues, and in 4.10–12 longevity, wisdom, virtue and security

---

[1] Zimmerli, *art. cit.*, p. 194.
[2] See E. Schmitt, *Leben in den Weisheitsbüchern Job, Sprüche und Jesus Sirach*, Freiburg, 1954, for a full discussion of this word.

The Ten Discourses and the Egyptian Instructions

are all linked together without distinction. To be good and to be happy appear to be identical in the mind of the teacher, who holds the key to both.

C. CONCLUSIONS

In the last section the remarkable similarity of the fundamental ideas of discourses and instructions was emphasized. This similarity is the more remarkable in view of the very great differences between Israelite and Egyptian religion and society.

As might be expected, these differences are reflected in the writings under discussion. The Israelite writer, for all his admiration of Egyptian educational methods, remained an Israelite writing for Israelites. In references to religion he never adopted any specifically Egyptian belief or vocabulary, but made use of that with which he was familiar. Thus in the discourses there is no trace of the Egyptian gods, no suggestion of polytheism and consequently none of the ambiguity about 'God' and 'the gods' which we find in the instructions. When a reference to God is needed it is, as a matter of course, the name Yahweh which appears. There is no reference to Egyptian mythology, but also none to the special characteristics of Yahwism. The Egyptian doctrine of the after-life which is occasionally referred to in the instructions has no place in the Israelite discourses.

These differences should not be regarded as deliberate omissions by the author of the discourses, for the discourses are not direct literary imitations of the instructions. Rather the discourses are representative of an early stage in the Israelite pedagogical tradition which, although in its origin it was closely related to the Egyptian, had from the first no need to borrow specifically religious ideas, which would have been repugnant to any Israelite, however closely he may have depended on Egypt for his culture.

But in fact these differences are minor, and do not weigh heavily in the balance against a theory of dependence of the Israelite wisdom tradition on the Egyptian. They are, of course, not minor in themselves—on the contrary, they concern religious beliefs of the greatest importance—but they are minor as far as the aim and theme of the instructions and discourses are concerned. Neither the Egyptian nor the Israelite authors were primarily interested in matters of religious belief and theology as such. These were matters which they claimed no competence to discuss, except by way of a general recommendation to their pupils not to forget their religious duties, by which they meant the duties prescribed by the established religion of their own country. They are much more concerned with the fundamental duty of conformity to a norm of behaviour which was not tied to any particular religion, and the knowledge of which they were confident of possessing through natural rather than supernatural means. The Israelite author's awareness and formulation of this norm was greatly assisted, if not created, by his own training in an educational system which was originally a foreign one; and basically it neither modified nor was modified by his religious beliefs as an Israelite, but rather existed in a parallel but distinct sphere.

It is perhaps significant that the author of the discourses, unlike his Egyptian counterpart,[1] makes no appeal to the antiquity of the tradition which he imparts. In Discourse V (4.4, 5b) he cites his own father's teaching in true Egyptian fashion, but he never speaks of this tradition as being more than one generation old. This is a material difference between discourses and instructions, and it may suggest that the discourses were written soon after the time when the scribal schools were first established. These Israelite teachers saw no need, or felt that it would be injudicious, to acknowledge openly their indebtedness to foreign teaching; in this they differed from the authors or editors of Prov. 30.1ff. and 31.1ff. This very rootlessness, which made it impossible for Israelite teachers to claim that their tradition was an ancient one, was one of the reasons why later generations tried to give increased status to it by associating it with the wisdom of Yahweh which existed from before the creation of the world.[2]

Another difference which has already been mentioned is that the teaching of the discourses is more general and less detailed than that of the instructions. Whereas the instructions are clearly intended to lay down specific principles of professional conduct and are addressed explicitly to young men destined for high office and social rank, the discourses are content to teach and

---

[1] E.g. *Ptahhotep* (Erman, p. 55); *Merikerē* (Erman, pp. 78, 79, 83); *Anii* (Erman, pp. 235, 236, 239). Cf. also the text for schoolboys, 'In Praise of Learned Scribes' (*ANET*, pp. 431f.).
[2] See ch. IV, *infra*.

The Ten Discourses and the Egyptian Instructions

illustrate general maxims applicable to life in general. The difference of aim is, however, more apparent than real. It is obvious from their contents that the discourses were not intended *by themselves* to be a complete system of education. They are exhortatory in character, and must have served as introductions to more detailed instruction. Some idea of the contents of the latter can be obtained from the material in Prov. 10–29, which contains many examples of specific teaching, some of which is quite professional in tone and remarkably similar to the professional teaching of the instructions.[1] If the discourses are regarded in this light, it becomes clear that they differ from the instructions only in scope and not in fundamental purpose.

Apart from the above points, none of which is of primary significance, no real difference is discernible between the fundamental ideas and aims of the discourses and those of the Egyptian instructions. Both were composed for use in the same kind of scribal school, an institution which the Israelites had borrowed, together with its curriculum, from the Egyptians.

The above comparison holds good only if chapter II's analysis of Prov. 1–9 into a book of educational discourses expanded by additional material is substantially correct. This analysis depends for its justification on three types of argument: literary analysis, the credibility of the Book of the Discourses as an example of a known literary form; and an adequate explanation of the motives for the addition of the remaining material in these chapters. The first two arguments have been presented in chapters II and III respectively. The third will be presented in the following chapter, and will form the basis for an understanding of the introduction and development of the figure of wisdom in the Israelite wisdom tradition.

[1] E.g. instructions on behaviour in the presence of kings and rulers, Prov. 14.35; 16.14f.; 20.2; 23.1–3; 25.6f., etc.

IV

THE DEVELOPMENT OF THE CONCEPT OF WISDOM

A. TWO TYPES OF WISDOM PASSAGE

THE theologically significant additions to the Ten Discourses in Prov. 1–9[1] are clearly distinguishable. They have not been added at random, but have been inserted at strategical positions: either into or immediately after the introductions to discourses, where they expand statements about the value and importance of the teacher's words, giving those statements a new meaning,[2] or between discourses where they give a new interpretation to the whole book.[3] In addition, a similar interpretative verse has been inserted between the Preface and the beginning of Discourse I (1.7), where it sets the theological tone for the whole book, and a long appendix has been added at the end of the book (chs. 8 and 9).[4]

A further glance at these additions, however, shows that they are not homogeneous. We are dealing here not with a single set of additions but with two distinct sets, each of which was made with a distinct theological purpose. In fact, there were two distinct stages in the process of the expansion of the discourses. The first set of additions was made directly to the discourses themselves; the second was never added directly to the discourses, but to the first additions, being either inserted into them or appended to them, and giving yet another interpretation to the book.[5]

---

[1] That is, material added or appended to the discourses to interpret or extend their teaching.
[2] 2.2–8, 10f. (II); 3.25f. (IV); 4.13 (VI); 6.23 (IX); 7.4 (X).
[3] 1.20–33; 3.13–20; 4.5a, 6–9.
[4] Disregarding 9.7–12, which has no particular theological significance.
[5] There is one exception to this. 1.7, which belongs to the second set, is added directly to the original Preface.

The Development of the Concept of Wisdom

The way in which the discourses have been expanded may be summarized as follows:

Preface (1.1–5)
  followed by 1.7 (group 2)

I. (1.8–19)
  followed by 1.20–33 (group 1)
    into which has been inserted 1.29 (group 2)

II. (2.1, 9, 16–19)
  including 2.2–4 (group 1)
    followed by 2.5–8 (group 2)
  also including 2.10f. (group 1)

III. (3.1–10)
  followed by 3.13–18 (group 1)
  followed by 3.19f. (group 2)

IV. (3.21–24, 27–32)
  No theological additions[1]

V. (4.1–4, 5b)
  followed by 4.5a, 6–9 (group 1)

VI. (4.10–12, 14–18)
  including 4.13 (group 1)

VII. (4.20–27)
  No additions

VIII. (5.1–6, 8, 21)
  No theological additions

IX. (6.20–22, 24, 25, 32)
  No theological additions[2]

X. (7.1–3, 5, 25–27)
  including 7.4 (group 1)
  followed by 8.1–21, 32–36 (group 1)
    into which have been inserted 8.13a (group 2) and 8.35b (group 2) and also 8.22–31 (group 2)

Concluding chapter: 9.1–6, 13–18 (group 1, but added later and showing some further developments)

[1] 3.26 is theological in the sense that it asserts that the real source of human confidence is God; but it does not belong to either of the main groups of addition, and may be simply a gloss.
[2] On 6.23 see p. 49, *supra*.

Wisdom in Proverbs

That these two groups are distinct can be demonstrated from both their literary form and contents. The passages in group 2 can be removed from the group 1 passages to which they are attached without any loss of grammatical coherence or metrical balance in the latter, and indeed their removal tends to improve both.[1] The sense is likewise not impaired but rather improved.[2]

The separation of these passages into two groups, one of which is attached to the other, reveals clearly the reasons for their addition to the discourses. The passages in group 1 are entirely concerned with something called 'wisdom'; and they have been added in such a way as to expand and interpret the teaching of the discourses by identifying wisdom—which is in some cases wholly or partly personified—with the purely human teaching of the discourses for which the teacher makes such absolute claims. This can be seen especially clearly in those passages which have been inserted into, or grammatically linked with, the discourses themselves. Thus in Discourse II the qualifying clause of v. 2 ('so that . . .'), the additional conditional clauses of vv. 3 and 4, parallel with v. 1, and the further qualifying clauses of vv. 10f. produce a sentence in which wisdom and the teacher's words are stated to be the same thing. In Discourse V 'get wisdom' (4.5) is made parallel to the 'keep my commandments' of the teacher in the previous verse. In Discourse X the addition of 7.4 achieves a similar purpose. The longer independent passages from this group which have been inserted between the discourses and at the end of the book serve the same purpose by somewhat different methods. The wisdom who in 1.20–28, 30–33 and 8.1–21, 32–36 stands in the public places of the city and addresses those who pass by speaks as a teacher offering instruction, and the benefits which she claims will accrue from following this instruction are the same as those offered by the teacher in the discourses.[3] Thus the impression is given that the person who addresses the pupil in the dis-

---

[1] Thus 2.5–8 seriously overload a sentence which the earlier addition of vv. 2–4 had already made cumbersome; and 8.13a is metrically superfluous.

[2] E.g. 1.29 introduces a new subject—the fear of Yahweh—into 1.20–33, but no further use is made of it in the verses which follow; 8.13a, 35b introduce a general statement about Yahweh into passages in which wisdom is speaking exclusively about herself; and 8.22–31 breaks into a passage in which wisdom is speaking of her gifts to men with a description of her origins.

[3] E.g. security (1.33), riches and honour (8.18); 'life' (8.35a).

courses is closely associated with wisdom. Similarly in 3.13-18, which is a poem describing the advantages of acquiring wisdom, wisdom and the words of the human teacher are by implication identified.

In all these passages wisdom is the central figure. But while the character, power and gifts of wisdom are described in detail, nothing is said about its origins. Never is it suggested that wisdom is of divine origin. God is never mentioned in connexion with it.

It was the main purpose of the passages in group 2 to supply this deficiency. In every one of these passages it is asserted that this mysterious wisdom of which the group 1 passages speak is Yahweh's wisdom. Three short interpolations into group 1 passages (1.29; 8.13a, 8.35b) assert, even at the expense of continuity of thought and regularity of metre[1] that wisdom and the 'fear of Yahweh' are inseparable and that to find wisdom is the same thing as to obtain Yahweh's favour. In 2.5-8 the same assertion is made and then strengthened by the positive statement: 'for it is Yahweh who gives wisdom' (v. 6). This is also clearly the purpose of 3.19f. and 8.22-31. 3.19f. is intended to explain the nature of the wisdom whose great value and benefits are so eloquently described in the group 1 poem 3.13-18: 'It is Yahweh who by wisdom founded the earth.' So also in 8.22-31, which begins with the words, 'It was Yahweh who created me. . . .'[2] In each of these last three passages the subject 'Yahweh' is placed at the beginning of the sentence, showing that it is here that the significance of these additions lies. So, too, in 1.7, the only place where a group 2 addition has been made directly to the text of the Book of Discourses. This verse, placed between the Preface (1.1-5) and the first discourse, is intended to set the tone for the whole book in its final form by asserting at the outset that whatever knowledge the pupil may acquire from it is in reality knowledge of Yahweh, whatever claims the human teacher may make:

[1] The metrical unit in these chapters is the distich. 8.13 has been made into a tristich by the interpolation of the first stichos. 8.35b is equally redundant, but the fact has been obscured by the present verse division, which makes v. 34 a tristich. The order of the stichoi of vv. 32-36 has been disturbed and should probably be rearranged as follows: 34a, 32b, 34b, c, 35a, 36a, omitting 32a and 33 as an extraneous fragment. (Nowhere else does wisdom speak of her 'sons'.) This arrangement restores the sense and the parallelism and shows that 35b is also an interpolation.
[2] See the discussion on the meaning of *qānānī* on pp. 100f., *infra*.

Wisdom in Proverbs

'It is reverence for Yahweh which is the essence of knowledge.'

Chapter 9 (i.e. vv. 1–6, 13–18, which originally formed a single unit) is not attached directly to the discourses and has a rather complex literary history of its own. But its point of view is basically the same as that of the group 1 passages in that its purpose is to recommend to a pupil the supreme importance of following the call of a wisdom whose virtues, in contrast with the specious attractions of 'the woman Folly' (v. 18), exist in their own right, without any suggestion that it is in any way related to God. This chapter may have been composed as a general conclusion to the book before the addition of the group 2 passages.

The motives for the twofold expansion of the Book of Discourses are thus reasonably clear. Each stage represents an attempt to re-interpret the teaching of the discourses. This recognition that the 'wisdom passages' in these chapters are of two distinct types makes possible a fresh approach to the old problems of the origin and motive of the figure of wisdom and of the development of the concept in Old Testament thought.

B. THE FIGURE OF WISDOM: FIRST STAGE

The questions to be considered here are the origin of the figure of wisdom in the group 1 passages, and the purpose for which it is introduced.

Some of the traits of the figure have been taken from phrases used in the discourses to describe the character and virtues of the teacher or his words. These features include the following:

1. The message given to the 'simple', i.e. the person who is as yet uninstructed, but who is also not yet hardened in the way of folly: 1.22; cf. 1.4; 7.7 in the discourses.

2. The claim that to heed wisdom is to obtain security in life: 1.32f.; 2.2; cf. 3.4; 3.21–24; 4.10–12.

3. The claim that the words of wisdom are righteous: 8.6–9, 20; cf. 2.1, 9; 4.10f.

4. The insistence on the incomparable value of wisdom's words: 3.13–15; 4.7f.; 8.10; cf. 1.8f.; 3.1–3; 4.22. (See further pp. 87f., *infra*.)

5. The claim to confer wealth, honour, long life, happiness, etc.: 3.16–18; 8.18, 21; 8.34a, 32b; cf. 3.2, 4; 4.10.

The Development of the Concept of Wisdom

6. The claim to confer (or to be) life itself: 4.13; 8.35a; 9.6; cf. 3.22; 4.22; 7.2.
7. The claim that wisdom enters the heart: 2.10; cf. 3.1, 3; 4.21; 6.21; 7.3.
8. The promise of wisdom to protect her followers: 2.11; cf. 3.24; 4.12.
9. The offer of a crown, garland, etc.: 4.9; cf. 1.9; 3.22.

In some cases wisdom and her gifts are described in precisely the same words as the gifts conferred by the teacher's words: the 'fair garland' which wisdom will place on the head of the young man who embraces her (4.9) is taken from 1.9; the admonition to 'guard her, for she is thy life' (4.13) from 3.21f.; 4.21f.

Other features of wisdom here may be traced to other figures in the discourses or to other Old Testament sources. Wisdom's character as a street preacher (1.20f.; 8.1–3) was probably inspired from four sources. The first is the character of the wisdom teacher, whose warnings are substantially the same as hers. Secondly the reference to the streets as the place where wisdom preaches was suggested by the references in the discourses to the moral dangers which face the young man in the streets, where he is tempted to fall into bad company, and more particularly, to yield to the temptations of the adulteress. Wisdom seems here to be presented as superior to the wisdom teacher because, while the latter remains (presumably) in the classroom, she descends into the arena and offers a challenge to evil where it is to be found. Thirdly the figure of the Hebrew prophet may have influenced the representation of wisdom as a preacher.[1] Fourthly the representation of wisdom as a woman whom the young man is urged to embrace and make his bride (4.6–9; 7.4) or who invites young men to her house (9.1–6) is partly designed as a contrast to the figure of the adulteress in the discourses.[2]

Yet when all these sources of literary inspiration have been

---

[1] Especially, as has been pointed out by Gemser (*ad loc.*), Robert (*art. cit.*, *RB* 43, pp. 172–81) and others, the speech of wisdom in 1.22ff. is reminiscent of the denunciations of the prophets both in contents and in the use of a number of characteristically prophetic phrases such as '*ad mātay*, 'how long?' (1.22; cf. Jer. 4.14, 21; Hos. 8.5, etc.) and *tāšūbū*, 'turn ye'. Wisdom's preaching in the 'broad places' also recalls the prophetic preaching (Jer. 5.1; 7.2).

[2] 7.4, where 'sister' is to be understood as meaning 'bride', as in Egyptian and in S. of S. 4.9–12; 5.1, is clearly intended to make a contrast (marriage as opposed to adultery) with the following verse about the adulteress. In 9.1–6,

taken into account, there still remain features of the figure which are unexplained; and above all the motive for its creation. The idea of wisdom as a person is entirely lacking in the discourses, and is certainly not to be derived from the Egyptian instructions, where the fundamental principle of *maat*, though personified and even deified in Egyptian religion, is never referred to in a way which offers a parallel with the figure of wisdom; and where the word *seboyet*, 'instruction', which is the nearest equivalent to 'wisdom', is never anything other than a common noun. Egyptian wisdom literature entirely lacks any personified abstract quality which could have given rise to the figure of wisdom.

There is no doubt that in Prov. 1–9 *in its present form* this wisdom is an attribute of Yahweh. This fact is not affected by the discussion of the extent to which it has developed into a distinct being or hypostasis. The main question at issue in the many discussions of this problem[1] is whether the hypothesis of its origin as the poetical personification of a divine attribute is sufficient to explain all the features of the passages in which it appears, or whether there is evidence of mythological influence, either foreign or native, in its origin or in its development. Those writers who have adopted the latter view have sought to identify the sources of this influence and to estimate its extent.

13–18 the figures of both wisdom and folly derive both their common feature (the appeal to young men to enter their house) and their essential antithesis (the results of the accepted invitation) from what is said in the discourses about the folly of adultery and the wisdom of avoiding it.

[1] Especially R. Reitzenstein, *Zwei religionsgeschichtliche Fragen*, Strasbourg, 1901, pp. 104–9; *Das mandäische Buch der Herrn der Grösse*, Heidelberg, 1919, pp. 53–55; *Das iranische Erlösungsmysterium*, Bonn, 1921, pp. 208–10; W. Schencke, *Die Chokma (Sophia) in der jüdischen Hypostasenspekulation*, Christiania, 1913; P. Heinisch, *Personifikation und Hypostasen im alten Testament* (Biblische Zeitfragen 9), Münster, 1921; *Die persönliche Weisheit des alten Testaments in religionsgeschichtlicher Beleuchtung* (Biblische Zeitfragen 11), Münster, 1923; R. Bultmann, 'Der religionsgeschichtliche Hintergrund der Prologs zum Johannes-Evangelium', *Eucharisterion, Studien zur Religion und Literatur des Alten und Neuen Testaments*, ed. H. Schmidt, vol. II, Göttingen, 1923, pp. 20f.; W. Bousset, *Die Religion des Judentums im späthellenistischen Zeitalter*, 3rd ed., ed. H. Gressmann, Tübingen, 1926, pp. 519f.; J. Fichtner, *Die altorientalische Weisheit*, pp. 118–28; Boström, *Proverbiastudien*; Rankin, *Israel's Wisdom Literature*, pp. 223–64; W. L. Knox, 'The Divine Wisdom' (*JTS* 38, 1937, pp. 230–7); Ringgren, *Word and Wisdom*, Uppsala, 1947, pp. 89ff.; G. von Rad, *Theology* I, pp. 441–53; W. Eichrodt, *Theologie des Alten Testaments*, 4th ed., vol. II, Göttingen, 1961, pp. 48–56.

The Development of the Concept of Wisdom

The analysis made at the beginning of this chapter of the wisdom passages in Prov. 1–9 into two distinct groups shows that it would be impossible to arrive at a solution of these problems by treating all the passages as if they were on the same level. It is also clear that in the Old Testament wisdom books there are other passages whose concepts of wisdom are different again from those in Prov. 1–9, especially Job 28 and other passages in Job such as 11.6ff.; 12.13; 15.7f.; 38.36f. It is now widely recognized[1] that the history of the figure of wisdom is a complex one. These differences cannot be explained by any simple theory of a development in a series of stages; they rather suggest that different writers experimented with the concept in different ways.

Even with the group of passages under discussion (the passages in group 1) there are differences in the treatment of the character of wisdom. She appears as a preacher only in 1.20ff. and 8.1ff.; she herself speaks only in 1.20ff.; 8.1ff.; 9.1ff.; her claim to authority over kings only occurs once (8.15f.); the themes of the house of wisdom, the seven pillars, the invitation to the feast and the contrast with the woman Folly only in 9.1ff. Moreover, while some of these passages appear to have been composed for insertion into the discourses, others (1.20ff.; 3.13–18; 8.1ff.) may have originally been independent poems which were inserted because they were considered appropriate to the context. Finally the *name* of wisdom appears in two different forms: the unusual form *ḥokmōt* in 1.20; 9.1 and the normal form *ḥokmā* elsewhere.[2]

These differences suggest that a number of different influences have been at work in the creation of the figure of wisdom. At the same time the various pictures all have certain features in common: wisdom is always spoken of as a being or object on whose possession or availability all human happiness depends; and in most passages it has the form and attributes of a woman.[3] These facts may, it would seem, best be accounted for by a theory of

[1] Especially by Ringgren (*op. cit.*, p. 89) and von Rad, *Theology* I, p. 441.

[2] The only two other occurrences of *ḥokmōt* in the Old Testament are Ps. 49.3; Prov. 24.7. For a discussion of the form and its significance see p. 85, *infra*.

[3] In the group 1 passages she is a woman preacher (1.20ff.; 8.1ff.); a bride (4.5a, 6–9; 4.13; 7.4); a hostess (9.1–6). Although three passages (2.2–4; 2.10f.; 3.13–18) do not state unequivocally that she is to be regarded as a woman, this may be inferred from their general similarity to the other passages. She is also clearly a woman in 8.22–31 (group 2).

some basic personification of a divine attribute to which the various writers have added mythological features taken from other traditions in order to give greater vividness to it. This is the conclusion reached by Ringgren in what is perhaps the most balanced study of the problem up to now.[1]

Many writers, however, have held that wisdom in all these passages is no more than a vivid poetical personification of an attribute of Yahweh virtually uninfluenced by mythological elements,[2] while others have maintained the opposite opinion that it is derived wholly or mainly from an originally independent goddess, one of whose attributes was wisdom, who under the influence of Yahwism lost her independent personality and was reduced to a subordinate status.[3] Each of these two types of theory, if maintained in a pure form, is unsatisfactory in that it fails to account for all the facts.

1. *The personification theory* The meaning of 'personification' in this context is the representation in personal terms of something which is not a person. In this sense wisdom is certainly personified in these passages, at least in 1.20ff.; 4.8f.; 8. The main purpose of personification is presumably to express in a vivid way the characteristics inherent in the thing personified. If the personification is confined to doing this, one may say of it that it has been carried out without the addition of features introduced from outside. There are other examples of such personification in the Old

---

[1] H. Ringgren, *op. cit.*, ch. 4. His conclusions are given on pp. 132f., 148. Similar conclusions had already been reached by earlier writers, especially Schencke, *op. cit.*, pp. 90–92. Cf. also Gemser, *op. cit.*, p. 5.

[2] So Toy, *op. cit.*, pp. xvii f.; E. Meyer, *Ursprung und Anfänge des Christentums* II, Stuttgart, 1921, p. 105; Heinisch, *op. cit.*; H. W. Robinson, *Inspiration and Revelation in the Old Testament*, Oxford, 1946, p. 269; W. A. Irwin, 'The Hebrews' in H. and H. A. Frankfort, *The Intellectual Adventure of Ancient Man*, Chicago, 1946, pp. 289f.; V. Hamp, *Das Buch der Sprüche* (Echter Bibel), Würzburg, 1949, p. 27; Renard, *Proverbes* (SB), p. 79; van der Ploeg, *Spreuken* (BOT), pp. 36–38; Sellin, *Alttestamentliche Theologie* I, p. 117. Others have admitted the possibility of such influence, but have minimized it.

[3] Reitzenstein found its origin in Hellenistic-Egyptian *Isis-Sophia* speculation; Bousset, followed by Rankin, in the Iranian *Amesha Spentas*; Hölscher in a combination of both. Schencke thought of the possibility of a re-emergence of an ancient native Israelite mythology; H. Gunkel, 'Sprüchebuch' (*RGG*[2] *V*, Tübingen, 1931, cols. 718–21) only of 'heathen mythology'. Boström, *op. cit.*, p. 174, held that the Babylonian *Astarte* was 'one of the roots' of the figure.

The Development of the Concept of Wisdom

Testament. In Ps. 85.10–13 'steadfast love' (*ḥesed*), 'truth', 'righteousness' and 'peace' are personified. These are all personifications of attributes of Yahweh. It is said of them that they 'meet', 'kiss', 'spring out of the earth', 'look down from heaven' and are sent to 'go before' Yahweh. All these metaphors are derived from the characteristics of these things themselves as attributes of Yahweh: they are aspects of his own character and so co-operate, both in heaven and on earth, in giving his gifts to men. Similarly in Ps. 89.15 God's attributes are said to be the foundation of his throne and to go before his face.[1]

But personifications of this kind are still in an embryonic state. They remain lifeless and relatively unimpressive because they lack positive features and a lively presentation. Such features can hardly be found within the character of the thing personified: they must be introduced from outside. This is an artistic necessity. In some of the personifications in the Old Testament—notably in Ezek. 23, where Samaria and Jerusalem are personified as two adulterous women—the personification takes the form of an allegory, and historical events and circumstances provide much of the necessary material, rendering the portraits lively and artistically interesting —though even here there is much poetic imagery which cannot be accounted for in this way, and which has clearly been borrowed from farther afield. But in the case of a divine attribute such as wisdom there is no such possibility. If wisdom was to be personified, she might take the form of a wise woman, as indeed she does, becoming a female teacher in 1.20ff.; 8.1ff.; but the possibilities end there. To make her into a lifelike and attractive person, which was clearly the intention of the author, additional features are needed.

In the polytheistic religions of the ancient near east the problem was solved by borrowing features from other deities. Characteristics passed easily from one god to another, especially in Egypt. Thus the Egyptian *Hu* and *Sia*, the 'creative word and the understanding of the high god *Rē-Atum* . . . attain so high a degree of independence that they can be associated with any other god'.[2]

---

[1] Cf. also Ps. 57.4; 61.8; 68.29. The possibility that some of these attributes may have been borrowed from Mesopotamian religion (Ringgren, *op. cit.*, pp. 150–5) does not affect the argument.
[2] Ringgren, *op. cit.*, p. 27.

In this way they acquired characteristics which completed their personalities and enabled them to be worshipped as distinct deities. Similarly the Egyptian *Hike*, 'magic', originally a minor divine attribute, acquired a complete set of mythological characteristics, and finally is represented as addressing the gods and informing them 'To me belonged everything, before ye gods came into existence.'[1]

The figure of wisdom in the Old Testament never came to be regarded as a deity independent of Yahweh. But it did achieve a degree of separateness from God; and it was natural that in this process it should have become invested with a number of additional features which are unrelated to its basic character as wisdom and as an attribute of Yahweh. To attempt to explain it *simply* as a personification which derived no features from outside is to postulate a phenomenon which was unknown[2] in the ancient near east, and to be faced with the impossible task of explaining a number of features—especially its representation as a woman attractive to young men—which are quite unrelated to the character of wisdom itself and which—as will be shown later[3]—bear a remarkable resemblance to foreign mythology.

2. *The mythological theories* On the other hand, theories which attempt to explain the origin of the figure wholly or mainly in terms of an originally independent mythological figure, whether foreign or Israelite, are also faced with insuperable difficulties. Whereas the theory that it is fundamentally the personification of an attribute of Yahweh—whatever other elements may have been added to it—is easily understandable, and is supported by similar later Jewish developments, such as the personification or partial personification of the Spirit, the Word and the Law, the appearance of a purely mythological female figure in the Old Testament would be inexplicable and unique. Mythological figures are notably absent from both Egyptian and Mesopotamian wisdom literatures, which are the product of the circles of the wise, to whom the cult—the locus of mythological traditions—was of

---

[1] *Ibid.*, pp. 29f.
[2] Except, as has been illustrated earlier, in the case of undeveloped or embryonic personifications.
[3] Pp. 89ff., *infra*.

little interest. It is unlikely that the Old Testament wisdom literature should be an exception.

But the strongest argument against the mythological theories in their pure form is provided by the very *name of wisdom*. Ringgren rightly pointed out that however strong the evidence for mythological features may be, 'such assumptions do not explain how personal Wisdom has originated. We get no explanation as to how a great goddess has become a relatively unimportant divine being *with an abstract name*.'[1] There is no trace in any of the Old Testament wisdom passages of her having possessed any other name than wisdom;[2] and no convincing evidence has been put forward for the substitution of the name 'wisdom' for the name of a deity. In the ancient near east, while there were gods and goddesses who were regarded as possessing the gifts of wisdom, there were none with that name. We must therefore conclude that wisdom in Proverbs is fundamentally a divine attribute which in the process of personification has been endowed with secondary mythological characteristics. The conclusion of Ringgren[3] that it originated from the belief, expressed in Isa. 31.2, that Yahweh is wise, seems inescapable.

3. *A Canaanite goddess of wisdom?* This conclusion has, however, been challenged by a group of scholars (notably W. F. Albright) who have put forward an entirely new theory which combines both the personification and the mythological theories.[4] They have argued that the origin of the figure of wisdom lies in the hypostatization of an attribute not of Yahweh but of the Canaanite high god *El*. It is therefore not originally an Israelite but a Canaanite figure which was introduced into Israelite wisdom literature in or before the seventh century BC, long after it had become a distinct goddess in Canaanite religion. Its first appearance in the Old Testament is in Prov. 1–9, especially in chapters

---

[1] *Op. cit.*, pp. 131f. Italics mine.
[2] Except for such equivalents as *bīnā*, 'understanding', used for the sake of parallelism. This usage is in any case rare in the passages where wisdom is personified, though common where it is used as a common noun.
[3] *Ibid.*, p. 132.
[4] W. F. Albright, *From the Stone Age to Christianity*, Baltimore, 1940, pp. 283f.; *Wisdom in Israel* (VT Suppl. 3), pp. 7f., 13; C. I. K. Story, 'The Book of Proverbs and North-west Semitic Literature', *JBL* 64, 1945, pp. 319–37, *et al.*

Wisdom in Proverbs

8 and 9, a document whose peculiar vocabulary and grammar show that it is of Canaanite, not Hebrew, origin. The Canaanite form of the name of this goddess has been preserved in the unusual and hitherto unexplained word ḥokmōt in 1.20; 9.1. The introduction of this figure constituted no threat to Hebrew monotheism: it was subordinated to Yahweh and interpreted symbolically. Some of its features had already been derived from other near-eastern wisdom deities. A reference in the Aramaic *Words of Aḥiqar* shows that it was also known outside Canaan in later times; but the real proof of its antiquity is provided by certain passages in the Ras Shamra Tablets.

This theory is attractive in that it claims to solve all the main difficulties concerning the origin of the figure of wisdom. It accounts both for the name 'wisdom' and for the mythological features, for although the Canaanite and Aramaic documents cited themselves contain few or no examples of mythological traits comparable with those in Prov. 1–9, Albright maintains that the Canaanite-Aramaean goddess called 'wisdom' replaced an older Canaanite goddess who possessed such mythological features.[1]

However, none of the three points on which the theory rests can be substantiated.

(*a*) With regard to the supposed Canaanite-Phoenician character of Prov. 8 and 9, the assertion that this 'gnomic document . . . swarms with words and expressions otherwise found only in such Canaanite texts as the Ugaritic tablets and the Phoenician inscriptions'[2] appears on detailed examination to be, at the least, an exaggeration,[3] and the thesis of the influence of Canaanite

---

[1] W. F. Albright, 'The Goddess of Life and Wisdom', *AJSL*, 1920, pp. 258–94; *From the Stone Age to Christianity*, pp. 284f.

[2] *From the Stone Age to Christianity*, p. 283. For detailed arguments see Albright in *Wisdom in Israel*, pp. 1–15, and Story, *art. cit.*, from which two articles the examples in note 3, *infra*, are taken.

[3] E.g. in 9.3, which according to Albright 'contains one grammatical peculiarity typical of Ugaritic . . . and three words characteristic of Ugaritic', the grammatical peculiarity (agreement of fem. sing. verb with plural antecedent) also occurs in Arabic and occasionally (though rarely with personal subjects, Jer. 50.10; Ezek. 25.10) in Hebrew; and of the three words in question (ʿal gappē, mᵉrōmē, qāret) only qeret, which is the normal Canaanite word for 'city' and very rare in Hebrew (though cf. Heb. qiryā and Syriac qrītā) can be considered a Canaanitism. mārōm is normal Hebrew, and gap, which occurs only once in Ugaritic and only here in Hebrew, is related to the Syriac geppā. Again the construction lᵉ in the sense of 'from' in 9.7 has now

The Development of the Concept of Wisdom

wisdom literature on these chapters is seriously weakened by the fact that no examples of that literature have come to light. Albright is forced to assume its existence.[1]

(b) Although it is possible that the form ḥokmōt in 1.20; 9.1, which is construed with a singular verb, is a Canaanite-Phoenician feminine singular form,[2] the vocalization of Phoenician cannot be regarded as settled beyond dispute,[3] and other explanations of ḥokmōt are given by competent scholars.[4] The view that we have here the actual name of a Canaanite wisdom goddess thus lacks sufficient proof.

(c) The argument of Albright depends principally, however, on the interpretation of four short passages in the Ras Shamra Tablets which contain the only six occurrences of the root ḥkm in extant Ugaritic literature.[5] All these refer to the wisdom of the

---

been recognized as normal Hebrew: C. H. Gordon, *Ugaritic Handbook* (Analecta Orientalia 25), Rome, 1947, pp. 81f. The words $q^e dōšim$ (9.10) and $r^e pā'īm$ (9.18) both occur in non-wisdom texts in the O.T. as well as here and in Ugaritic literature. Other examples of the same kind could be given.

[1] Thus 'It would be very strange if the North-West Semites of Syria and Palestine did not share in the high appreciation of didactic literature ... which we find in Egypt and Mesopotamia'; 'It is most unreasonable to assume that didactic literature appeared any later in Syria-Palestine than in any other ... area' (*ibid.*, pp. 3f.).

[2] *Ibid.*, p. 8, following a suggestion of H. L. Ginsberg based on the statement of J. Friedrich, *Phönizisch-Punische Grammatik* (Analecta Orientalia 32), Rome, 1951, sections 78, 213, 227, 228, that this was pronounced '—ōt'.

[3] The fem. sing. may, in fact, have been pronounced '—at'. The few extant examples where a vowel-letter is used (bʿl ʿnwt and ʿnwt, quoted in A. Dupont-Sommer, 'Une Stèle Araméenne d'un prêtre de Baʿal trouvée en Egypte', *Syria* 33, 1956, p. 84, n. 1) may be dialectal. The only occurrence of the word ḥkmt in an inscription from Karatepe (M. Dunand, 'Une nouvelle Version des Inscriptions Phéniciennes de Karatépé', *Bulletin du Musée de Beyrouth* 8, 1946–8, p. 21; col. 1, line 13 in the text) in the form bḥkmty 'in my wisdom' gives no indication of the pronunciation.

[4] According to E. Brønno, *Studien über hebräische Morphologie und Vokalismus*, Leipzig, 1943, pp. 187f., it is a mistaken pointing for the normal plural $ḥ^a kāmōt$; H. Bauer and P. Leander, *Historische Grammatik der Hebräischen Sprache des Alten Testaments*, Halle, 1922, section 61, consider it to be a normal, though rare, Hebrew singular form and thus simply an alternative to ḥokmā; and the view of C. Brockelmann, *Grundriss der vergleichenden Grammatik der semitischen Sprachen* II, Berlin, 1913, section 29b, that it is an irregular 'plural of majesty or excellence' has been followed by several recent commentators.

[5] Keret II, iv, 2; Baal V, v, 30f.; II, iv, 41f.; II, v, 3f. (G. R. Driver, *Canaanite Myths and Legends*, Oxford, 1956, pp. 42, 90, 96).

Wisdom in Proverbs

high god *El*. From these passages, especially from one, which he translates 'The wise El has attributed to thee (O Baal) wisdom (*ḥkmt*), together with eternity of life and good fortune',[1] Albright draws the conclusion that at Ugarit there was a 'glorification of wisdom' which was the origin of the 'Canaanite-Hebrew hypostatized Wisdom' of Prov. 1–9.[2] Such a conclusion is unwarranted. That a high god like *El* should himself be wise, and should be able to confer wisdom on others, is not at all extraordinary; but that that wisdom was regarded as a personal being distinct from its possessor is nowhere stated.[3]

The other text on which Albright relies is equally unable to support the weight of his thesis. This is a passage from the Aramaic *Words of Aḥiqar*, dated by Albright about the sixth century.[4] Assuming the correctness of the restorations and translation of these lines accepted by Albright, it is said here that[5] '(wi)sdom is (from) the gods, and to the gods she is precious; for (ever) her kingdom is fixed in heav(en), for the lord of the holy ones (i.e. the gods of heaven) hath raised her'. Here there is undoubtedly a hypostatization of wisdom which in some ways is parallel to some of the passages in group 1 of Prov. 1–9, though it is doubtful whether the view that behind it lies 'some romance concerning an older goddess of Wisdom'[6] whom wisdom herself has replaced can be substantiated. However, it is difficult to understand in what way this sixth-century *Aramaic* text supports the thesis of a *Canaanite* influence on the figure of wisdom in Prov. 1–9. This hypostatization of wisdom may be quite unconnected with the development of the concept in Old Testament wisdom literature.[7]

We may conclude that there is a similarity of ideas in *Aḥiqar* and Proverbs, but in the absence of more direct evidence of a common source or of an ancient and continuous tradition of a hypostatized wisdom in the ancient near east in which the authors

---

[1] Baal II, iv, 41f.
[2] *From the Stone Age to Christianity*, p. 283.
[3] Even Ringgren's statement that 'it would seem as if *El*'s wisdom was becoming at least a kind of objective entity which might be the starting-point of a hypostatization' (*op. cit.*, p. 80) is an exaggeration.
[4] Lines 94f. Text in Cowley, *op. cit.*, p. 215.
[5] Quoting Albright, *loc. cit.*
[6] Story, *art. cit.*, p. 335; cf. Albright, *op. cit.*, p. 284.
[7] This appears to be the opinion of Ringgren, *op. cit.*, pp. 147f.

The Development of the Concept of Wisdom

of the wisdom passages in Prov. 1-9 shared, there is no reason to suppose that the personification in Proverbs was not in origin a native Israelite phenomenon.

4. *Supposed mythological features* The rejection of all the above theories leaves only one possibility: that the figure of wisdom is a genuine Israelite personification of an attribute of Yahweh, which in its extended poetical expression in the group 1 passages in Prov. 1-9 has attracted to itself a number of traits, added for practical, didactic or descriptive purposes, which are, strictly speaking, irrelevant to the nature of wisdom itself.[1] It has been maintained that some of these traits have been derived from non-Israelite mythological material generally familiar to the peoples of the ancient near east. They are of four main kinds.

(*a*) *Wisdom as an object of incomparable value, to be sought and obtained at all costs* (2.4; 3.13-15; 4.5a, 7, 13; 8.10, 19, 35a, 36b) The language here used goes beyond what is said in the discourses about the value of the teacher's words, and is very emphatic. The vocabulary is distinctive. Wisdom must be diligently sought for (2.4; 8.35a), purchased (4.5a, 7), grasped and guarded (4.13; 8.10). It is compared to gold, silver and other precious objects (2.4, 3.14f., 8.10, 19); but the profit which its possessor obtains from it is greater than any of these (3.14f.; 8.10, 19). It is life itself (3.18; 8.35a).[2] In some of these passages it is not clear whether wisdom is thought of as an object to be acquired or as a woman to be sought as a bride; in others it is clear that she is a woman. The theme is not peculiar to Prov. 1-9, but is found also in a single short statement in Prov. 16.16, and again in an expanded form in Job 28.15-19.

A mythological background has been proposed for these passages; but there is some disagreement about the identity and

[1] For the reason why its relation to Yahweh is concealed in these passages see pp. 92ff., *infra*.

[2] The expression '*ēṣ ḥayyim* (3.18), which also occurs in Prov. 11.30; 13.12; 15.4, is translated by most commentators 'tree of life', and connected with Gen. 2.9; 3.22-24. If this is the correct meaning, there is probably a mythological reference here. But more probably the phrase means '*staff* of life', since the context and especially the verbs *tāmak*, 'grasp' and *heḥeziq*, 'take hold of' are inappropriate to the meaning 'tree'. '*ēṣ* has the meaning 'stick, staff' in II Sam. 21.19; 23.7; II Kings 6.6; Ezek. 37.16ff., and perhaps elsewhere.

87

character of this myth. For some writers it is a myth of the theft of wisdom from the gods, perhaps by the 'Primeval Man' (*Urmensch*);[1] others relate it to the descent of Ištar into the underworld and her subsequent elevation,[2] to the *Isis-Osiris* myth[3] or to an otherwise unknown myth of a being with magical powers whom Yahweh had to seek out and find in order to obtain her assistance in the creation of the world.[4] Whatever plausibility there may be in this theory as applied to Job 28 and Prov. 8.22-31, where wisdom's association with creation is asserted,[5] a mythological explanation is not required in the case of the group 1 passages in Prov. 1-9.[6] The characteristic comparison with precious objects in these passages probably originally had no connexion with wisdom but was used in ordinary life. Thus in Prov. 31.10 it is used of the 'good wife': 'A good wife who can find? She is far more precious than corals.'[7] Prov. 16.16, where similar language is used about wisdom but with no elaboration and no suggestion of personification, may mark an intermediate stage in the process whereby a well-known form of speech came to be applied to wisdom and eventually to be elaborated in a poetical manner. The simple observation of the advantages which have accrued to men who possessed wisdom, rather than a mythological figure, probably lies behind these passages.[8]

[1] Schencke, *op. cit.*, pp. 7-10, and A. Weiser, *Das Buch Hiob* (ATD 13), 1956.
[2] Bultmann, *art. cit.*
[3] W. L. Knox, *art. cit.*, pp. 233f.
[4] P. Volz, *Hiob und Weisheit* (Die Schriften des Alten Testaments, ed. H. Gunkel, III/2), 2nd ed., Göttingen, 1921, p. 114. G. Hölscher, *Das Buch Hiob* (HAT), 1937, pp. 65f., considered that there is mythological influence in Job 28, but was uncertain about the identity of the myth.
[5] Some writers deny mythological influence in Job 28 also: Ringgren, *op. cit.*, pp. 94f.; C. Westermann, *Der Aufbau des Buches Hiob* (Beiträge zur historischen Theologie 23, Tübingen, 1956), pp. 104-7; von Rad, *Theology* I, pp. 446f.; N. H. Tur-Sinai (H. Torczyner), *The Book of Job, A New Commentary*, Jerusalem, 1957, p. 248.
[6] It may also be noted that Job 28.15-19, which closely resembles the group 1 passages, has been held by a number of scholars (Budde, Hölscher, Schencke, Lindblom, Westermann) to be an addition to the chapter with a different theme: the value, rather than the inaccessibility, of wisdom.
[7] Cf. Prov. 3.15; 8.11; Job 28.18.
[8] Another non-mythological explanation, not incompatible with the above, may be found in the suggestion of Westermann (*op. cit.*, pp. 104-6), that Job 28 is to be explained as a literary development of the answer to the question—originally a riddle—'Where is wisdom to be found?': a question derived

The Development of the Concept of Wisdom

(*b*) *Wisdom as directing the government of kings and rulers* (8.15f.) No mythological explanation is required for this passage, though various foreign deities are credited with the same powers.[1] Throughout the ancient near east wisdom was regarded as a special prerogative of kings, and Israel was no exception, as is shown by the tradition of Solomon's wisdom, especially I Kings 3.4–15 and Isa. 11.2.[2] Here the gift of government which elsewhere is said to be given by God in his wisdom is attributed to a personified wisdom which, although in accordance with the character of the group 1 passages this is not stated, is, in fact, an attribute of his and not derived from any external source.[3]

(*c*) *The personification of wisdom as woman and as bride* (4.6, 8f.; 7.4) Here the young man is advised to embrace and love wisdom and to make her his bride.[4] It has been argued by Boström that behind these features of wisdom stands the figure of *Astarte*, the goddess of love, whose worship in various forms and under various names was widespread in the countries of the ancient near east. But this mythological influence is an indirect one. The figure of wisdom itself was created as a symbol of the cult of Yahweh,[5] in order not to encourage but to oppose the influence of a foreign sexual cult of *Astarte* which was attracting the young Israelites of the time. But in order that wisdom should make an effective appeal to these young men as a rival to *Astarte*, the author of these passages depicted it as a woman and invested it with some of the

---

from the observation that it is a rare commodity. This suggestion is particularly apposite with regard to Job 28, but may also have influenced the other passages, inasmuch as precious stones and objects are not only valuable but hard to get. On the early stages of the development of wisdom see von Rad, *Theology* I, pp. 418–41.

[1] E.g. *Ištar*. See J. Plessis, *Etude sur les textes concernant Ištar-Astarté*, Paris, 1921, p. 57; Boström, *Proverbiastudien*, p. 173.

[2] For other references see Gemser, *op. cit.*, p. 1.

[3] It may be noted that the verse preceding this passage (8.14) corroborates this theory. This verse, in which wisdom claims absolute possession of counsel, 'sound wisdom', understanding and strength, seems to have been modelled on Job 12.13, where the same qualities are said to belong to God.

[4] References to marriage include the 'garland' or 'crown' worn by the bridegroom (S. of S. 3.11; Isa. 61.10; cf. Isa. 28.5; 62.3) and the use of the word 'sister' (7.4) as bride, as in S. of S. 4.9–12; 5.1. There may also be a reference to a wedding-feast in Prov. 9.1–6 (Boström, *op. cit.*, pp. 160f.).

[5] *Op. cit.*, pp. 156, 174.

characteristics of *Astarte* herself. Some of these were borrowed from the descriptions of the 'strange woman' against whom the young man is warned elsewhere in Prov. 1-9,[1] whom Boström interprets as a representative of the foreign women who try to lure the young men into participation in the sexual cult; others can be identified as attributes of *Astarte-Ištar* by comparison with pagan literature concerning the goddess of love and the women who practised her cult. Among these is the character of the bride.[2] The self-praise of wisdom in Prov. 8 is reminiscent of the hymns in which *Ištar* glorifies herself.[3] The fact that *Ištar* was also worshipped as goddess of wisdom[4] may have provided a starting-point for the attribution of these features to the figure of wisdom.

Some of the detailed arguments of Boström, especially concerning the meaning of the 'strange woman' and the supposed foreign sexual cult, have failed to carry conviction[5] and have been incisively criticized, especially by Humbert;[6] but his contention that *Astarte* is one of the sources of the figure of wisdom[7] remains extremely probable.

(*d*) *The building of the house with seven pillars* (9.1) The apparently simple statement that 'Wisdom has built her house, she has hewn out (or 'set up')[8] her seven pillars' has been interpreted by a number of writers as a reference to an ancient cosmic myth. Reitzenstein,[9] following a clue from the Mandaean literature, found here a reference to the great temple of Babylon, the 'house of the foundation of earth and heaven', which represented the world and which, according to Herodotus, consisted of seven towers built one on top of another. The building of the seven-pillared house by wisdom thus referred, like Prov. 8.22-31, to her creative activity,

---

[1] 2.16-19; 5.3ff.; 6.24ff.; 7.5ff.
[2] *Ibid.*, pp. 161-8.
[3] *Ibid.*, p. 173.
[4] *Ibid.*, pp. 170f.
[5] See, e.g., Gemser, *op. cit.*, p. 5.
[6] P. Humbert, 'La "femme étrangère" du Livre des Proverbes', *RES* 6, 1937, pp. 49-64; 'Les adjectifs "Zâr" et "Nokri" et la "femme étrangère" des proverbes bibliques', in *Mélanges Syriens offerts à M. René Dussaud* I, Paris, 1939, pp. 259-66.
[7] *Ibid.*, p. 174.
[8] Some commentators, following LXX, emend *ḥāṣᵉbā* to *hiṣṣîbā* as giving a more probable sense.
[9] *Mandäische Buch*, pp. 53-56; *Zwei . . . Fragen*, pp. 208-10.

The Development of the Concept of Wisdom

and was part of a hellenistic Jewish polemic against certain Babylonian-Iranian cosmological conceptions, in which Jewish wisdom was endowed with some of the characteristics of the foreign 'false wisdom' which is represented elsewhere in Prov. 1–9 by the 'strange woman'. Boström[1] also worked out a cosmological interpretation of the seven pillars, partly based on Reitzenstein, according to which the seven pillars represent the seven planets, and are connected with the Babylonian cult of the Queen of Heaven, '*Ištar* of the Stars', and thus constitute a further example of *Ištar*-traits in the figure of wisdom.[2]

The cosmological theories about the meaning of this apparently straightforward verse derived much of their plausibility from the widely-held belief that the lack of archaeological evidence about pillared houses in or near Palestine made a literal interpretation of Wisdom's seven-pillared house out of the question. Since then the discovery of remains of Phoenician houses of the late third millennium with roofs supported by seven interior pillars,[3] when combined with literary evidence of pillared buildings both religious and secular from later times,[4] has made it likely that the seven pillars are merely a concrete detail taken from ordinary life added to give vividness to the scene.[5] The number seven may be intended to signify perfection, or may merely indicate that the house was an unusually spacious one. There may also be an allusion here to the 'house of instruction' or school of which there is evidence for a later period (*bēt midrāšī*, Ecclus 51.23). There is therefore no need for cosmological or mythological interpretations here.

---

[1] *Op. cit.*, ch. 1.

[2] For another theory of an ancient cult involving the use of seven pillars, see W. F. Albright, 'The Archaeological Results of an Expedition to Moab and the Dead Sea', *BASOR* 14, 1924, p. 10; 'Two Great Discoveries bearing on the Old and New Testaments', *BASOR* 58, 1935, pp. 13ff.; *Wisdom in Israel* (VT Suppl. 3), p. 8.

[3] M. Dunand, 'La Maison de la Sagesse', *Bulletin du Musée de Beyrouth* 4, 1940, pp. 69–84.

[4] E.g. the House of the Forest of Lebanon (I Kings 7.2–7); Sennacherib's New Year Festival House (*bit akitu*) at Asshur whose pillars were arranged in rows of seven (B. Meissner, *Babylonien und Assyrien* I, Heidelberg, 1920, p. 308; W. Andrae, *Das wiederstandene Assur*, Leipzig, 1938, pp. 32ff., 151–3).

[5] So, among recent commentators, Gemser, *op. cit.*, 2nd ed., 1962; van der Ploeg.

Wisdom in Proverbs

We may then conclude that of the various features of the figure of wisdom in the group 1 passages which are not directly related to the basic character of wisdom as a divine attribute many were derived from material in the discourses or simply from the poetical imagination of the author; but that one—her representation as a female figure who speaks in praise of herself and is to be embraced as a bride—shows the influence of the figure of the goddess of love *Ištar-Astarte*. But there is no suggestion of polytheism here, nor of a process whereby a formerly independent goddess has lost her status and become a lesser spiritual being subordinate to Yahweh. The mythological features are secondary and not systematically presented. The parallels and contrasts between the figures of wisdom and of the woman Folly in 9.1-6, 13-18, and between these two figures and the 'strange woman' of Discourses II, VIII, IX and X show that one of the motives for wisdom's representation as a woman was to present the pupil with an attractive alternative to the 'strange woman'. If Boström's theory of a sexual cult is untenable and the woman simply represents the ordinary temptation of adultery,[1] then this motive was a purely didactic one with no special religious significance. It was natural that in the polytheistic and syncretistic milieu of the ancient near east, where even in Israel the cult of the goddess of love cannot have been entirely unfamiliar, this theme should have expressed itself partly in her imagery.

5. *The purpose and function of the wisdom passages* But the dismissal of the mythological features as secondary does not wholly solve the problem of the passages in group 1. Two important questions remain: *why* the discourses were expanded by the addition of passages which equate the words of the wisdom teacher with a personified wisdom;[2] and why no explicit mention is made in those passages of the connexion of this wisdom with God.

The very fact that the additions were made indicates that those who made them considered the discourses to be unsatisfactory, or at least in some way inadequate, yet believed that, properly inter-

---

[1] As Humbert has convincingly argued in the two articles referred to on p. 90, n. 6, *supra*.
[2] The argument in the previous paragraph does not answer this question, as it is concerned only with the addition of feminine traits to an *already* personified wisdom.

The Development of the Concept of Wisdom

preted, they contained valuable teaching. The inadequacy lay most probably in the fact that, although the discourses contained nothing which was positively opposed to the Israelite religious or social tradition, and had to some small extent modified the thought and expressions of their Egyptian models in conformity with Israelite ways of thinking, there was in them an underlying ethos which, though hardly expressed in words, remained alien. This was not so much their negative view of God as their static view of life and their claim to an absolute authority. For the Israelite, life in all its aspects was understood in terms of action and change;[1] and motives for conduct, in so far as they were higher than the ordinary human appetites, were understood in terms of the positive command of the living God who actively participated in the events of history. The Israelite reaction to a doctrine of an immutable, self-existent and impersonal order would be not so much rejection as incomprehension. The authority claimed on the basis of this order would consequently also be misunderstood; and the attitude of the prophets to the wise men show that this was so. Unlike the prophet and the priest, the wisdom teacher made no claim to divine authority, yet he asserted that only by following his admonitions could a man find happiness and prosperity, and that to neglect them was to court disaster. This claim was virtually the same as that which was made in the Yahwistic tradition for the Word of Yahweh,[2] and must have appeared to many to be setting up a new kind of authority over the lives of Israelites as a challenge to that of Yahweh. It was this which provoked the condemnation of human wisdom in the pre-exilic prophets,[3] but which also led to the search for a means of reconciliation between the two traditions. It has been suggested earlier[4] that the basis of the reconciliation is contained in the formula that 'He (Yahweh) also is wise' (Isa. 31.2). This proved

---

[1] See T. Boman, *Hebrew Thought Compared with Greek*, London, 1960, pp. 49–51. However valid may be the criticisms of Boman's methods by J. Barr, *The Semantics of Biblical Language*, Oxford, 1961, pp. 50–54, his general position remains valid, especially in contrast to the Egyptian conception of the world.

[2] Especially in the prophetical books. It is summarized in such passages as Deut. 30.11–20 in words which, *mutatis mutandis*, are not unlike those in which the authority of the wisdom teacher is expressed.

[3] See pp. 21f., *supra*.

[4] P. 23.

ultimately to be the most satisfactory means of reconciliation. To identify the *word* of Yahweh with the word of the wisdom teacher might seem to be the most obvious means, but it was unthinkable to identify a new and alien tradition with a concept which was so fundamental to Yahwism, and so to raise the wise men to a status of equality with the prophet as official mouthpieces of Yahweh. The idea of Yahweh's *wisdom*, on the other hand, was relatively undeveloped and had none of the associations which were attached to the idea of his word, and so was relatively innocuous.

Thus the purpose of both groups of additions to the discourses was fundamentally the same: to bring the wisdom tradition represented by the discourses into relation with Israelite ways of thought and to give it a place—though not the supreme place—within Yahwism. The audience for whom these additions were intended was still, however, the young pupil in the schools; and by representing wisdom in a lively fashion as a living and active person the author hoped to give additional force to his teaching.

Thus in both groups of wisdom passage the wisdom which is so highly commended is, in fact, Yahweh's wisdom; but the two groups represent two different stages in the process of integration. When the first group was added it was not yet possible to state the relation between Yahweh and wisdom unequivocally: there can be no other explanation of this reticence. To what extent those who read or heard the Book of the Discourses in its first revised edition (with the first group of additions only) fully understood what was implied it is difficult to say. 'Wisdom' was a common noun expressing an attribute which was human as well as divine,[1] and was used quite apart from the specialized literature of wisdom in the sense of 'skill' or 'shrewdness', with no specific reference to God; yet at the same time men recognized in a general way that, like all other human qualities, it was a gift of God. In emphasizing the connexion of the words of the teacher of the discourses with this 'wisdom' with which every Israelite was familiar, the author of these passages found a means of making the discourses less alien to the Israelite reader, yet without making his meaning so precise as to arouse the opposition of the official guardians of the Yahwistic tradition.

We should therefore interpret the figure of wisdom in these

[1] E.g. 'my wisdom' referring to the teacher, Prov. 5.1.

The Development of the Concept of Wisdom

passages as marking a first and tentative stage in the 'nationalization' or 'theologizing' of wisdom: a first attempt to reconcile two different traditions. At the same time the figure, enlivened by feminine traits drawn partly from foreign sources, provided the pupil in the Israelite wisdom schools with an incentive to 'embrace' their instruction which was not afforded by the somewhat cold appeals of the teacher.

C. THE FIGURE OF WISDOM: SECOND STAGE

The passages in group 2 represent a later stage in the process of assimilation. The fact that they are all (with the exception of 1.7) appended to group 1 passages indicates that their purpose was to supplement the latter. Their emphatic statements that wisdom—and therefore, by implication, the teaching of the discourses—comes from Yahweh show that the assimilation of the two traditions was now far advanced, and could be expressed in direct terms. Although these passages are clearly earlier than Ecclesiasticus, where some of the implications of this new theological position are worked out further,[1] their standpoint is not essentially different from that expressed by Ecclesiasticus when he sums up the history of the wisdom tradition accurately from the Jewish point of view by making wisdom say that she first dwelt with every nation, but was finally commanded by God to 'take root' permanently in Israel, where she served before God and possessed authority in Jerusalem (24.6–12), or when he defines the wisdom of the wise man as a human skill acquired by diligent study of both the 'law of the Most High' and the 'wisdom of the ancients', and as directed by God and sustained by prayer (39.1–8). They are theological rather than polemical, providing positive teaching about the relation between Yahweh and wisdom, making clear what was previously only implied. This relationship is shown in two main ways: by the identification of wisdom with the 'fear of Yahweh' and by the assertion of the antiquity of wisdom's association with God.

1. *The 'Fear' of Yahweh* Of the seven passages in this group, four (1.7; 1.29; 2.5; 8.13a) identify wisdom with the 'fear' or

---
[1] See Ringgren, *op. cit.*, pp. 106–13.

Wisdom in Proverbs

'reverence' (*yir'ā*) of Yahweh. This phrase is mainly confined to the wisdom literature, of which it is a characteristic expression.[1] It occurs five times in almost identical phrases defining the nature or essence of wisdom or knowledge.[2]

An examination of the use of the verb 'to fear' (*yārē'*) and the noun 'fear' (*yir'ā*) in connexion with Yahweh shows that this concept, like that of wisdom, was closely associated with *education*. The two phrases 'wisdom' and 'fear of Yahweh' signify two originally distinct types of education in Israel: the teaching of the wisdom schools and the ordinary religious education of the Israelite given by parents or by the religious authorities.

When used in connexion with the word 'God', 'fear' (both verb and noun) referred to a standard of moral conduct known and accepted by men in general. Thus Abraham, distrusting the 'moral atmosphere' of Abimelech's court, said 'The fear of God is not in this place' (Gen. 20.11). On the other hand, the midwives refused to kill the Israelite babies because they feared God (Ex. 1.17, 21). With respect to particular gods, this 'fear' embraces every aspect of reverence towards them, including both worship (II Kings 17.35) and obedience (II Kings 17.7f.). The fear of Yahweh (mainly expressed through the verb rather than in the phrase *yir'at* Yahweh) likewise included these meanings;[3] but owing to the special character of Yahweh it has some unique characteristics. These are most clearly expressed in II Kings 17, where the fear of Yahweh *ipso facto* excludes the service of other gods and is closely associated with the Covenant (vv. 38f.). In Deuteronomy (10.12f.) it is closely associated not only with obedience to Yahweh but also with love for him.

The concept of 'fearing Yahweh' thus included every aspect of Israel's relationship to him: obedience, loyalty, worship, sacrifice and love. Indeed, it appears to be this phrase which most nearly expressed what modern scholars call Yahwism (or Judaism). It is

---

[1] Excluding equivalents (e.g. 'thy fear' used of Yahweh) and the phrase 'the fear of God', which has a wider meaning, it occurs eighteen times in the wisdom books and wisdom psalms and only in four other places (II Chron. 19.9; Isa. 11.2, 3; 33.6).

[2] Job 28.28; Ps. 111.10; Prov. 1.7; 9.10; 15.33.

[3] Avoidance of evildoing, Neh. 5.9, 15; Prov. 10.27; 16.6, etc.; worship, Ps. 34.12; II Kings 17.36, etc.; obedience to Yahweh's commandments, Lev. 19.14, 32; 25.17; Deut. 4.10; 5.29; 6.2, etc.

The Development of the Concept of Wisdom

in this sense that Obadiah used it when he said to Elijah, 'I thy servant fear Yahweh from my youth' (I Kings 18.12).

But in order to understand the significance of the passages in the wisdom literature which assert that wisdom (or knowledge) is to be found principally in the fear of Yahweh it is important to observe the close connexion of the phrase with *education*. In the instructions of Deuteronomy and the 'Holiness Code' (Lev. 17–26) the frequent occurrence of the injunction to fear Yahweh indicates its connexion with religious instruction; and in a number of passages the fear of Yahweh is to be taught and learned (Ps. 34.12ff.; Deut. 17.18–20). In II Kings 17.25–28 the Assyrian deportees living in the cities of Samaria were attacked by lions sent by Yahweh because they did not know *how* (*mišpāṭ*) to fear Yahweh, and these attacks ceased only when a priest was sent to 'teach them how they should fear Yahweh' (v. 28).

This connexion between education and the fear of Yahweh appears in an important prophetic passage (Isa. 29.13f.) in which it appears that the wise men were taking upon themselves the instruction of the people, not only in traditional wisdom, but in religious matters as well:

> And Yahweh said: Because this people draw near with their mouths, and honour me with their lips, but their heart is far from me, and their fear of me is (only) a commandment of men which has been taught them, therefore . . . the wisdom of their wise men shall perish, and the understanding of their discerning men shall be hidden.

Thus in Isaiah's time the attempt of the wisdom teachers to include in their curriculum that religious instruction which was properly the prerogative of the priests was condemned as mere human teaching resulting in a superficial, and therefore worthless, knowledge of Yahweh. It is, however, significant that the attempt to bridge the gap between wisdom and Yahwism was made by the wisdom teachers as early as the time of Isaiah, even though the motives were misunderstood by the prophet.

The situation had evidently already radically changed when the latest additions to Prov. 1–9 were made. From these it appears that the wisdom schools had now succeeded in their endeavour to unify the two systems of education. It was now possible in those schools to make the bold assertion which stands at the beginning of the book (1.7) that the very essence of knowledge—such as formed their traditional curriculum (1.2–5)—is the fear of Yahweh, that is, the practice of the religion of Yahweh in all its aspects. The Preface in its revised form (1.2–5, 7) announces the syllabus of the wisdom school in its two distinct yet now inseparable aspects.

From that time onwards the formula of 1.7 (which is echoed in 1.29; 2.5; 8.13a) became a kind of motto or statement of principle, testifying to the new 'orthodox' status of the wisdom teacher and his school. It was added to other parts of Proverbs (15.33; 9.10) and to Job 28 (v. 28), bringing those wisdom texts 'up to date'. When Ecclesiasticus was written it was still in use (1.14).

2. *The divine origin of wisdom* The assertion that the ancient wisdom tradition and the revealed knowledge of Yahweh are compatible and complementary is supported by three further passages which state plainly in more theological language that all wisdom comes from Yahweh. The first of these (2.6) is a simple statement: 'For it is Yahweh who gives wisdom; from his mouth come knowledge and understanding.'[1] This statement is further elaborated in two other passages (3.19f.; 8.22–31) which refer to the role of wisdom in creation. The latter of these two passages is a much more elaborate composition than the former, and its style and form have been suited to the context into which it has been inserted (a speech of self-praise by a personified wisdom) but they both serve the same purpose: to assert in the strongest terms possible the great antiquity and importance of the wisdom taught in the schools. Both introduce the name Yahweh emphatically at the outset and stress the antiquity of his close association with wisdom, implying that if wisdom was precious to Yahweh from the beginning of the world, it is impossible to doubt its infinite value to men.[2]

---

[1] 2.1–6 is interesting in that here the whole literary history of Prov. 1–9 is epitomized. The original teacher's personal claim to authority is first re-interpreted as an invitation to acquire a most precious but undefined 'wisdom' (vv. 2–4), and this is then further defined as something which comes directly from Yahweh (vv. 5f.).

[2] Cf. the remark of G. Wildeboer (*Sprüche* [KHAT], 1898) with regard to 8.22–31, that Wisdom here 'shows the patent of her nobility'.

The Development of the Concept of Wisdom

3.19f. is a brief statement about the creation of the world, similar to statements in the Psalms and prophets.[1] Appended to a group 1 passage (3.13–18) in which wisdom is commended rather as a precious object than as a person, these verses which speak of its relation to Yahweh also refrain from speaking of it in unequivocally personal terms.[2]

In 8.22–31, where wisdom is clearly represented as a person in conformity with the context, the purpose is clearly the same. The many difficulties of interpretation of particular words in this passage do not obscure the fact that great emphasis is placed on the *priority in time* of wisdom as the associate of Yahweh. This is stated in every verse from v. 22 to v. 30. In vv. 23–26 wisdom asserts that she was present with Yahweh *before* any of his works of creation was performed.[3] In verses 27–30a it is again stated that wisdom was already there when the acts of creation were performed. Like 3.19f. this poem is appended to a statement about the preciousness of wisdom. That which is old is precious; and so, as Gemser pointed out, the extreme antiquity of wisdom (as well as her connexion with Yahweh) is put forward as a guarantee of her ability to confer the gifts which she has promised to confer in the preceding verses.

Although the purpose of the insertion of 8.22–31 is the same as that of 3.19f., the personification of wisdom here, which is as highly developed as it is in those group 1 passages where wisdom is described as a woman and a bride, raises the question whether mythological elements have played their part in the process. The answer to this question depends to a large extent on the interpretation of certain words, especially *qānānī* (v. 22), *nissaktī* (v. 23), *ḥōlāltī* (vv. 24, 25), *'āmōn* (v. 30), the first three of which refer to the way in which wisdom came into existence, while the fourth defines the role which she played at Yahweh's side during the

---

[1] For the phrase 'founded the earth' (*yāsad 'ereṣ*) cf. Ps. 78.69; 102.26; 104.5; Job 38.4; Isa. 48.13, etc. 'Established' (*kōnēn*) is used several times in the same sense, and in Ps. 24.2 in parallelism with *yāsad* as here.

[2] There may be a partial, or undeveloped personification here. Cf. Ps. 104.24; 136.5. In these passages the personification has gone little farther than in Isa. 48.13, where it is Yahweh's 'hand' which founded the earth.

[3] No less than five words denoting temporal priority are used: *miqqedem*, *bĕ'ēn*, *bĕṭerem*, *lipĕnē*, *'ad-lō'*. This unparalleled emphasis on temporal priority makes it probable that the much discussed *rē'šīt* and *qedem* in v. 22 should also be interpreted in a temporal sense.

creation of the world. The meaning of these words has been the subject of much discussion.

1. *qānānī*. This word describes the manner in which Yahweh brought wisdom into existence, and so may be thought to indicate the author's view of her nature; but its precise meaning has been in dispute since ancient times.[1] It has been variously translated as 'created me', 'possessed me', 'acquired me', 'begot me'. All these translations have been defended by modern commentators. It may be questioned, however, whether it is legitimate to draw any far-reaching theological conclusions from the philological debate. The basic meaning of the verb appears to be to 'acquire';[2] and most if not all the subsidiary meanings express particular ways of acquiring (buying, begetting children, etc.) or the result of acquisition (possession of a thing). Recent discussion[3] has concentrated mainly on the question whether the meaning 'create' is possible. Although most of the Old Testament and Ugaritic passages cited in support of this meaning[4] are susceptible of other interpretations, it can hardly be denied that the meaning 'form, create' gives the only possible sense in at least one Old Testament passage.[5] But it is doubtful whether a rigid distinction should be made between the meanings 'beget' and 'create', since, unless we are to believe that Yahweh is here said to be a 'father' in the sense in which, e.g. *El* becomes a father by a sexual act in the poem of *Shachar and Shalim*[6]—which would be unparalleled in the Old

---

[1] The Versions are divided between 'acquired' or 'possessed' (Aquila, Symmachus, Theodotion, Vulgate) and 'created' (LXX, Peshitto, Targum).

[2] C. F. Burney, 'Christ as the APXH of Creation', *JTS* 27, 1925–6, pp. 161–3.

[3] G. Levi Della Vida, 'El 'Elyon in Genesis 4.18–20', *JBL* 63, 1944, pp. 1–9; P. Humbert, ' "Qānā" en Hébreu biblique', *Festschrift für Alfred Bertholet*, Tübingen, 1950, pp. 259–66 (reprinted in P. Humbert, *Opuscules d'un Hébraïsant*, Neuchâtel, 1958, pp. 166–74); Albright, *Wisdom in Israel* (VT Suppl. 3), pp. 7f.; W. A. Irwin, 'Where Shall Wisdom Be Found?', *JBL* 80, 1961, pp. 133–42.

[4] Gen. 4.1; 14.19, 22; Ps. 78.54; Baal II, i, 20 (G. R. Driver, *Canaanite Myths and Legends*, p. 92).

[5] In Ps. 139.13, where it is meaningless for the Psalmist to say that Yahweh 'acquired' or 'possessed' his kidneys, and probably in Deut. 32.6, where the verb is parallel with 'made' and 'established', and is at least a metaphor for creation even if it literally means 'begot' here. The translations of LXX and other Versions also show that this meaning was known in ancient times.

[6] Driver, *Canaanite Myths and Legends*, pp. 120–5.

The Development of the Concept of Wisdom

Testament—the meaning 'begot' here must be figurative and so equivalent to 'created'.

In view of the context of Prov. 8.22–31, which is concerned with God's creative activity, the meanings 'acquired me' or 'possessed me' for *qānānī* are improbable, and we should therefore translate either 'created me', or 'begot me' in the metaphorical sense of 'created'. Thus no real distinction is made between the manner of the formation of wisdom and of the other works of creation. The point of this verse, as of the succeeding verse, is merely that wisdom was created *first*.

2. *nissaktī*. This word, although it is parallel with *ḥōlaltī*, 'I was born', in the following verse, has frequently been interpreted as referring, not to wisdom's creation but to her appointment by God to a high rank or office.[1] This interpretation is based on the meaning of the verb *nsk* in Ps. 2.6 and the noun *nāsīk*,[2] 'prince, leader'. But in view of the parallelelism it is more probable that the word is derived from another word meaning 'to weave',[3] and that it is used metaphorically of the process of conception. If this be so, there is no reference here to wisdom's activity in creation but only to her own birth, that is her creation.

3. *ḥōlaltī*. 'I was brought forth (in labour).' Like *qānānī* (if it is translated 'begot') and *nissaktī*, this word is used figuratively, as in Deut. 32.18, where God is said to be the Rock who begot (*yālad*) Israel and the God who gave him birth (*meḥōlēl*). These metaphors of birth require no mythological explanation: they are part of the personification of wisdom in this chapter and are merely poetical language.

4. *'āmōn*. This word, which occurs, vocalized in this way, in only one other passage in the Old Testament, where also its meaning is disputed,[4] is a well-known *crux interpretationis*, and has

[1] So e.g. Ringgren, *op. cit.*, p. 102: 'The passage means ... that Wisdom possessed from the beginning royal or divine dignity.'

[2] Jos. 13.21; Ezek. 32.30; Micah 5.4; Ps. 83.12; cf. Accadian *nasiku*, which has the same meaning.

[3] Possibly from *skk*, *śkk*, used of the formation of the foetus in the womb, Ps. 139.13; Job 10.11 (by changing the vowels and reading *nesakkōtī*), or more probably, with no vowel-changes, from *nsk*, a by-form of *skk* which occurs in Isa. 25.7; 30.1 and in the noun *massēkā*, 'woven stuff'.

[4] Jer. 52.15, where 'the rest of the *'āmōn*' are listed among the groups of

been made to bear considerable theological weight. It has been thought to be an Accadian loanword meaning 'craftsman';[1] and on the basis of this interpretation it has been maintained that wisdom is here represented as participating actively with Yahweh in the creation of the world. Some scholars have gone farther and maintained, with the aid of a 'mythological' interpretation of such other words as *qānānī* ('begot me') and *nissaktī* ('I was given divine rank') and of an interpretation of Job 28.23–27 according to which God 'searched for' and 'found' wisdom, without whose masterly knowledge he could not have made the world,[2] that an originally independent mother-goddess lies under the surface of the whole passage. The meaning 'craftsman' is, however, by no means certain, and the view, which was already apparently held by Aquila, that the word means 'nursling'[3] and refers to wisdom's being a young child when the word was created, fits well with the words 'delight' and 'playing' in the same verse. Other interpretations have also been proposed.[4]

It is unlikely that certainty will be reached on this question. The context, however, lends probability to the view that *'āmōn* should be translated in a non-active sense. Nowhere else in the poem is there any suggestion of independent creative activity on the part of wisdom. Verses 22–29 are concerned solely with the antiquity of her association with God, and it is repeatedly stated that it is he who created all things. Whatever interpretation should be given to the words 'delight' (*ša'ašū'īm*) and 'playing' (*mᵉšaḥeqet*)

---

people sent into exile by the Babylonians. But in a parallel text II Kings 25.11 has *hāmōn*, 'commotion, multitude', which is also not satisfactory, and in another reference to the same event Jer. 39.9 has *'ām*, 'people'. Jer. 52.15 is omitted in LXX.

[1] Acc. *ummānu*. This is certainly the meaning of *'ommān* in S. of S. 7.2. The form *'āmōn* might be due to a misunderstanding of the pronunciation of a foreign word, and would give tolerable sense in Jer. 52.15.

[2] For these views see Volz, *Hiob und Weisheit*, p. 114; D. Nielsen, *Die altsemitische Muttergöttin* (ZDMG 92), 1938, p. 550; Hölscher, *Hiob* (HAT), pp. 65f.; Schencke, *Die Chokma*, pp. 11–15.

[3] Either vocalizing *'āmūn* (Qal passive participle from *'āman* 'to nurse', which occurs in Lam. 4.5), or as a noun *'ᵉmūn*. Gemser suggested that even with its present vocalization it might be an adjective having the same meaning.

[4] See R. B. Y. Scott, 'Wisdom in Creation: the 'Āmōn of Proverbs VIII 30', *VT* 10, 1960, pp. 213–23.

The Development of the Concept of Wisdom

in vv. 30f.,[1] they also contain no allusion to creative activity. If the author of the poem had intended to represent wisdom as a divine being who assisted actively in the creation of the world it is highly improbable that he would have made the single word *'āmōn* bear the whole burden of his meaning.

But even if 'craftsman' *is* the true translation of *'āmōn*, it would not necessarily indicate mythological influence. A 'master craftsman' is not necessarily an architect. He is a skilled worker whom one would normally expect to be under superior orders. Wisdom is undoubtedly personified here as in the rest of chapter 8, but the poem 8.22–31 is no more than an expansion, in personified terms, of the statement in 3.19 that 'Yahweh founded the earth *by* wisdom'.[2]

There is thus nothing in these words which suggests a mythological origin for wisdom; and this is equally true of the passage as a whole. The terms used to describe wisdom's origin are metaphorical, not mythological, and the single word which can be interpreted as speaking of her *activity* at the Creation does not essentially go beyond the statement of 3.19. Everything which is here said about her can be naturally interpreted as belonging properly to the poetical personification of an attribute of Yahweh, the purpose of which is to emphasize its extreme antiquity. This is not to say that this passage shows no trace of external literary influence. It may have been adapted from some otherwise nonextant account of creation,[3] but if such an account had contained references to a creatrix- or co-creatrix-goddess, one would expect clearer traces of this to have been left. It is more natural to suppose that a creation narrative in which there is a single creator-god has been adapted to fit the chapter into which it has been inserted by

---

[1] Especially whether these are to be regarded as the activity of a child or have some deeper significance.

[2] It may be noted that the Aramaic equivalent of the Accadian *ummānu* was used as the title of a royal official, i.e. a subordinate person (S. Smith, 'An Inscription from the Temple of Sin at Ḥuraiḏha in the Ḥaḏhramawt', *BSOAS* 11, 1945, p. 456).

[3] Gemser pointed out a resemblance in the syntax and content of vv. 23–26 with the Egyptian *Apophis*-myth (*ANET*, p. 6) and the Babylonian *Enuma Eliš* (*ANET*, pp. 6of.) and Gen. 1.1f.; 2.5, which may point to a widespread common literary form for creation stories.

the addition of the theme of the self-praise of that wisdom which is the subject of the original part of the chapter.

Although it may be that in this passage the association of wisdom with Yahweh has carried its hypostatization farther than it is carried in any other passage in the Old Testament, it was not the intention of the author to indulge in cosmological speculation such as we find in the Wisdom of Solomon and in later Gnostic writings, but simply to commend the teaching of the wisdom schools by showing how closely it was associated with Yahweh and the fear of Yahweh. This is shown by the fact that 8.22–31 was not placed at the end of the book to form its climax. This editor (the editor of the passages in group 2) left 9.1–6, 13–18, in their final position, so that it was still this final, dramatic appeal by wisdom, contrasted with the appeal of Folly, which summed up the book. 8.22–31, although it has been considered by most modern writers to be the highest point in the teaching of the book, was not so considered by its author, who intended it merely to fulfil an auxiliary function similar to that of 3.19f.

Thus when it has been assigned to its proper place in the structure of Prov. 1–9, 8.22–31 ceases to be a major problem. The hypostatization of wisdom as an attribute of Yahweh was carried out here not in order to bridge the gulf between God and man which had been created by the increasing tendency of orthodox Judaism to regard God as wholly transcendent,[1] but to bridge another gap—that between the wisdom tradition and the main Israelite religious tradition—by emphasizing that all wisdom comes from God. This purpose was partly fulfilled by the addition to the discourses of the passages which we have called 'group 1', in which the wisdom of the schools was represented as an object of infinite value to be acquired at all costs and personified, with some assistance from mythological motifs, as a virtuous woman to be embraced as a bride. It was completed, without the addition of any further mythological motifs, by the 'group 2' passages in which wisdom was identified with the practice of the religion of Yahweh and, more directly still, with that immemorial wisdom of Yahweh which he exhibited when he created heaven and earth.

[1] Bousset, *Die Religion des Judentums*, pp. 342f.

V

EPILOGUE

APART from its limited objective of re-investigating the origin and purpose of the figure of wisdom in Prov. 1–9, the foregoing study has perhaps succeeded in shedding a little light on the wider problem of the history of the wisdom tradition in Israel, which is still by no means completely elucidated.[1] The strongly Egyptian character of the Book of the Ten Discourses, despite their Israelite dress, and the two successive attempts to re-interpret them in terms of categories more acceptable to the Israelite mind, the first of which was tentative and cautious, tend to confirm the view, already put forward on other grounds, that the process of assimilation was a long one which began before the Babylonian Exile had, by reason of the external pressures to which it exposed them, forced the Jews to synthesize their various traditions as a matter of urgency. The ambiguous character of the first re-interpretation suggests that when it was made the issue had not yet been decided: just as in another sphere the relation of Yahweh to the world of nature was still the subject of polemic up to the time of the Exile,[2] so also the question whether all the works of the human mind, including those educational, political and cultural spheres in which the Israelites were so greatly indebted to the heathen but vastly superior Egyptians, were to be regarded as nevertheless the gift of Yahweh alone was still a matter of debate. It may be asserted with some confidence that this state of affairs, which the new analysis of Prov. 1–9 reflects, corresponds to the period of the great pre-exilic prophets, two at least of whom participated in the debate.

The second group of additions, which appear to have been

---

[1] Cf. the recent statement by von Rad (*Theology* I, p. 441): 'We have no means of bridging the great gulf between Prov. 10–29 on the one hand and Prov. 1–9 on the other.'

[2] E.g. Jer. 44.17f.

made when the issue had been decided, must for this reason be assigned to the post-exilic period. It is not possible to assign them a precise date, but they contain nothing which certainly indicates hellenistic influence. The arguments that they show the influence of Greek philosophy or speculation which once had a certain plausibility[1] have been undermined by an increased knowledge of older Egyptian and Semitic sources which already express certain ideas previously believed to have originated with the Greeks. The controversial word 'ēṭūn (7.16), even if it is a Greek loanword (ὀθόνη), does not necessarily point to a hellenistic date, since it may have been borrowed long before the hellenistic period in the course of trade. The marked difference between the development of the hypostatization of wisdom in Prov. 8 and in Ecclesiasticus also suggests that these latest passages in Prov. 1–9 should be assigned to the Persian period.

As theological statements, the passages in which it is asserted that Yahweh created the world by his wisdom are of the first importance quite apart from the relatively limited purpose which they were intended to fulfil. For in stating the creative activity of Yahweh in this form they greatly enriched the possibilities of the development of the implications of that doctrine. The other statements of this doctrine in the Old Testament (Gen. 1; 2; Deutero-Isaiah) were made primarily in the context of the history and worship of the Chosen People, and, though they invite admiration of the Creator, show no interest in the questions which man might want to put about the complexities of the world around him. The author of Gen. 2 ('J'), whose main interests lay elsewhere (in the relationships between God and man and between man and woman), was content to speak of the creation itself in the language of the ancient myths; for 'P' it was the transcendent and incomprehensible 'word' of God which caused the world to come into being.[2] The hymn-like language of Deutero-Isaiah is intended to call forth praise for the Creator and to emphasize the insignificance of man in comparison with him. But the statement that Yahweh

---

[1] E.g. J. Hempel, *Die althebräische Literatur und ihr hellenistich-jüdisches Nachleben*, Potsdam, 1930, pp. 191–3; W. L. Knox, *art. cit.*, *JTS* 38, p. 236; H. W. Robinson, *Inspiration and Revelation*, pp. 248, 259f.
[2] See von Rad, *Theology* I, pp. 139ff.

Epilogue

created the world by *wisdom* provides for the first time the possibility of relating the whole of man's intellectual curiosity about the world, whether expressed confidently, as in the discourses of Prov. 1–9, or in terms of frustration, as in Job 28.1–22, to the Israelite belief in the supreme lordship of Yahweh. For the whole tenor of Prov. 1–9 in its present form is that the wisdom which is available, through education, to those who are willing to learn and to fear Yahweh and through which a man may acquire the ability to steer his course safely through this complex and dangerous world is essentially the same as the wisdom through which that world was originally created, and that it is a gift from Yahweh himself. Through this formula later Judaism was able to resolve the opposition between man's intellectual curiosity, previously regarded with suspicion as leading to pride and rebellion against God, and God's sovereignty, and so to construct a reasonable faith which could be commended to the outside world.

SELECT BIBLIOGRAPHY

COMMENTARIES ON PROVERBS

COHEN, A., *Proverbs* (The Soncino Books of the Bible), London and Bournemouth, 1952
DELITZSCH, F., *Das Salomonische Spruchbuch* (Biblischer Commentar über die poetischen Bücher des Alten Testaments III), Leipzig, 1873
DUESBERG, H. AND AUVRAY, P., *Le Livre des Proverbes (SBJ)*, Paris, 1957
FRANKENBERG, W., *Die Sprüche* (Handkommentar zum Alten Testament, ed. by W. Nowack), Göttingen, 1898
GEMSER, B., *Sprüche Salomos* (HAT), Tübingen, 1937; 2nd ed. 1962
GREENSTONE, J. H., *Proverbs*, Philadelphia, 1950
HAMP, V., *Das Buch der Sprüche* (Echter Bibel), Würzburg, 1949
JONES, E., *Proverbs and Ecclesiastes* (Torch Bible Commentaries), London, 1961
NOWACK, W., *Die Sprüche Salomos* (Kurzgefasstes exegetisches Handbuch zum Alten Testament), Leipzig, 1883
OESTERLEY, W. O. E., *The Book of Proverbs* (Westminster Commentaries), London, 1929
PLOEG, J. VAN DER, *Spreuken* (BOT), Roermond, 1952
RENARD, H., *Le Livre des Proverbes* (SB), Paris, 1951
RINGGREN, H., *Sprüche* (ATD), Göttingen, 1962
SCHNEIDER, H., *Die Sprüche Salomos* (Herders Bibelkommentar), Freiburg, 1962
STRACK, H. L., *Die Sprüche Salomos* (Kurzgefasster Kommentar zu der Heiligen Schriften des Alten und Neuen Testaments), Munich, 1899
TOY, C. H., *A Critical and Exegetical Commentary on the Book of Proverbs* (ICC), Edinburgh, 1899
VOLZ, P., *Hiob und Weisheit (Das Buch Hiob, Sprüche und Jesus Sirach, Prediger)* (Die Schriften des Alten Testaments III/2), 2nd ed., Göttingen, 1921
WIESMANN, H., *Das Buch der Sprüche* (Die Heilige Schriften des Alten Testaments), Bonn, 1923
WILDEBOER, G., *Sprüche* (KHAT), Leipzig, 1898

EGYPTIAN AND SEMITIC TEXTS AND TRANSLATIONS

COWLEY, A., *Aramaic Papyri of the Fifth Century B.C.*, Oxford, 1923
DRIVER, G. R., *Canaanite Myths and Legends*, Oxford, 1956

Select Bibliography

ERMAN, A., *The Literature of the Ancient Egyptians*, translated by A. M. Blackman, London, 1927
GLANVILLE, S. R. K., *The Instruction of 'Onchsheshonqy (Catalogue of Demotic Papyri in the British Museum* II), London, 1955
GRIFFITH, F. LL., 'The Teaching of Amenophis, the son of Kanekht', *JEA* 12, 1926, pp. 191–231
LAMBERT, W. G., *Babylonian Wisdom Literature*, Oxford, 1960
LEXA, F., *Papyrus Insinger: Les enseignements moraux d'un scribe égyptien du premier siècle après J.-C.*, Paris, 1926
PRITCHARD, J. B. (ed.), *Ancient Near Eastern Texts Relating to the Old Testament*, Princeton, 1950; 2nd ed., 1955
VOLTEN, A., *Das Demotische Weisheitsbuch* (Analecta Aegyptiaca 2), Copenhagen, 1941

OTHER WORKS

ALBRIGHT, W. F., 'Some Canaanite-Phoenician Sources of Hebrew Wisdom', *Wisdom in Israel and in the Ancient Near East. Presented to H. H. Rowley* . . . (VT Suppl. 3), Leiden, 1955, pp. 1–15
ALT, A., 'Die Weisheit Salomos', *TLZ* 76, 1951, pp. 139–44 = *Kleine Schriften zur Geschichte des Volkes Israel* II, Munich, 1959, pp. 90–99
ANTHES, R., *Lebensregeln und Lebensweisheit der alten Ägypter* (Das Alte Orient 32, Heft 2), Leipzig, 1933
BAUMGARTNER, W., 'Die israelitische Weisheitsliteratur', *Theologische Rundschau* N.F. 5, 1933, pp. 259–88
BOSTRÖM, G., *Proverbiastudien: Die Weisheit und das fremde Weib in Spr. 1–9*, Lund, 1935
BRUNNER, H., *Altägyptische Erziehung*, Wiesbaden, 1957
'Die Weisheitsliteratur', *Handbuch der Orientalistik*, ed. by B. Spuler, vol. I, Part II, Leiden, 1952, pp. 90–110
DE BOER, P. A. H., 'The Counsellor', *Wisdom in Israel* (VT Suppl. 3), 1955, pp. 150–61
DRIVER, G. R., *Semitic Writing from Pictograph to Alphabet* (Schweich Lectures, 1944), London, 1948
DUESBERG, H., *Les Scribes Inspirés* I, Paris, 1938
DÜRR, L., *Das Erziehungswesen im Alten Testament und im Antiken Orient*, Leipzig, 1932
FICHTNER, J., *Die altorientalische Weisheit in ihrer israelitisch-jüdischen Ausprägung: eine Studie zur Nationalisierung der Weisheit in Israel* (BZAW 62), Giessen, 1933
FRANKFORT, H., *Ancient Egyptian Religion: An Interpretation*, New York, 1948
GALLING, K., *Die Krise der Aufklärung in Israel*, Mainz, 1951
GESE, H., *Lehre und Wirklichkeit in der alten Weisheit*, Tübingen, 1958

Select Bibliography

HUMBERT, P., *Recherches sur les sources égyptiennes de la littérature sapientiale d'Israël*, Neuchâtel, 1929

LINDBLOM, J., 'Wisdom in the Old Testament Prophets', *Wisdom in Israel* (VT Suppl. 3), 1955, pp. 192–204

VON RAD, G., *Old Testament Theology* I, Edinburgh and London, 1962, pp. 418–53

RANKIN, O. S., *Israel's Wisdom Literature*, Edinburgh, 1936

RANSTON, H., *The Old Testament Wisdom Books and their Teaching*, London, 1930

RINGGREN, H., *Word and Wisdom: Studies in the Hypostatization of Divine Qualities and Functions in the Ancient Near East*, Uppsala, 1947

ROBERT, A., 'Les attaches littéraires bibliques de Prov. I–IX', *RB* 43, 1934, pp. 42–68, 172–204, 374–84; 44, 1935, pp. 344–65, 502–25

RYLAARSDAM, J. C., *Revelation in Jewish Wisdom Literature*, Chicago, 1946

SCHENCKE, W., *Die Chokma (Sophia) in der jüdischen Hypostasenspekulation: Ein Beitrag zur Geschichte der religiösen Ideen im Zeitalter des Hellenismus*, Kristiana, 1913

SCOTT, R. B. Y., 'Solomon and the Beginnings of Wisdom in Israel', *Wisdom in Israel* (VT Suppl. 3), 1955, pp. 262–79

SKLADNY, U., *Die ältesten Spruchsammlungen in Israel*, Göttingen, 1962

WÜRTHWEIN, E., *Die Weisheit Ägyptens und das Alte Testament*, Marburg, 1960

ZIMMERLI, W., 'Zur Struktur der alttestamentlichen Weisheit', *ZAW* 51, 1933, pp. 174–204

INDEX OF AUTHORS

Albright, W. F., 19f., 30, 83ff., 91, 100, 109
Alt, A., 9, 20, 109
Andrae, W., 91
Anthes, R., 54, 60, 109
Auvray, P., 25, 30, 34, 39, 41, 43, 108

Barr, J., 93
Bauer, H., 85
Baumgartner, W., 66, 109
Begrich, J., 18
Bentzen, A., 19
Bertram, G., 64
Blackman, A. M., 9, 109
Boer, P. A. H. De, 18, 109
Boman, T., 93
Boström, G., 50, 78, 80, 89f., 91, 109
Bousset, W., 78, 80, 104
Breasted, J. H., 54
Briggs, C. A., 9
Bright, J., 28
Brockelmann, C., 85
Brønno, E., 85
Brunner, H., 16, 25, 35, 45, 52, 53, 54, 55, 57, 60, 109
Buck, A. de, 25, 54
Budde, K., 88
Bultmann, R., 78, 88
Burney, C. F., 100

Causse, A., 31
Clamer, A., 10
Cohen, A., 34, 108
Cowley, A. E., 9, 46, 51, 86, 108

Dahood, M., 42
Delitzsch, F., 33, 108
Della Vida, G. L., 100
Drioton, E., 16

Driver, G. R., 35, 40, 42, 46, 47, 85, 100, 108, 109
Driver, S. R., 9, 30, 34
Duesberg, H., 25, 30, 34, 39, 41, 43, 108, 109
Dunand, M., 85, 91
Dupont-Sommer, A., 85
Dürr, L., 19, 109

Eichrodt, W., 78
Eissfeldt, O., 9, 34
Erman, A., 9, 15f., 18, 35, 36, 38, 39, 51, 53, 55, 56, 58, 59, 60, 70, 77, 109

Fichtner, J., 30, 78, 109
Finkelstein, L., 30, 40
Frankenberg, W., 108
Frankfort, H., 25, 54, 55, 80, 109
Frankfort, H. A., 80
Friedrich, J., 85

Galling, K., 20, 29, 109
Gemser, B., 20, 33, 34, 38, 39, 40, 41, 43, 44, 46, 52, 53, 80, 89, 90, 91, 99, 102, 103, 108
Gese, H., 25, 52, 55, 62, 109
Gesenius-Kautzsch, 9, 40, 46
Ginsberg, H. L., 85
Glanville, S. R. K., 53, 109
Gordon, C. H., 85
Greenstone, J. H., 108
Gressmann, H., 25, 78
Griffith, F. Ll., 16, 109
Grossouw, W., 9
Gunkel, H., 42, 80, 88

Hamp, V., 34, 80, 108
Heinisch, P., 78, 80
Hempel, J., 106
Herntrich, V., 9

Index of Authors

Hölscher, G., 80, 88, 102
Humbert, P., 37, 38, 51, 90, 92, 100, 110

Irwin, W. A., 80, 100

Jones, E., 108

Kahle, P., 9
Kamphausen, A., 33
Kittel, R., 9
Klostermann, A., 19, 34
Knox, W. L., 78, 88, 106
Koehler, L., 66

Lambert, W. G., 35, 38, 51, 109
Leander, P., 85
Lexa, F., 25, 109
Lindblom, J., 21, 22, 88, 110

Marti, K., 10
Meissner, B., 91
Meyer, E., 80
Montgomery, J. A., 23

Nielsen, D., 102
Noth, M., 28
Nowack, W., 108

Oesterley, W. O. E., 30, 34, 38, 40, 41, 43, 44, 108
Ooert, H., 42

Pfeiffer, R. H., 27, 30, 34
Pirot, L., 10
Plessis, J., 89
Ploeg, J. van der, 34, 38, 40, 80, 91, 108
Plummer, A., 9
Pritchard, J. B., 9, 109

Rad, G. von, 11, 15, 21, 78, 79, 88, 89, 105, 106, 110
Rankin, O. S., 25, 78, 80, 110

Ranston, H., 30, 110
Reitzenstein, R., 78, 80, 90, 91
Renard, H., 34, 39, 40, 41, 43, 48, 80, 108
Ringgren, H., 78, 79, 80, 81, 83, 86, 88, 95, 101, 108, 110
Robert, A., 16, 25, 26, 37, 51, 77, 110
Robinson, H. W., 80, 106
Rylaarsdam, J. C., 30, 110

Schaeder, H. H., 28
Schencke, W., 78, 80, 88, 102, 110
Schmidt, H., 78
Schmitt, E., 68
Schneider, H., 108
Scott, R. B. Y., 20, 23, 102, 110
Sellin, E., 25, 30, 80
Skladny, U., 20, 24, 25, 27, 110
Smith, S., 103
Spuler, B., 25, 109
Stock, H., 57
Story, C. I. K., 83, 86
Strack, H. L., 34, 108
Stummer, F., 31

Thomas, D. W., 39, 47
Torczyner, H., see Tur-Sinai, N. H.
Toy, C. H., 29f., 39, 40, 43, 44, 45, 47, 49, 80, 108
Tur-Sinai, N. H., 88

Vaux, R. de, 18
Volten, A., 25, 109
Volz, P., 31, 43, 88, 102, 108

Weiser, A., 9, 88
Westermann, C., 88f.
Wiesmann, H., 108
Wildeboer, G., 33f., 40, 98, 108
Würthwein, E., 25, 62, 64, 110

Zimmerli, W., 63, 64, 65, 68, 110

INDEX OF BIBLICAL REFERENCES

Genesis
1	106
1.1f.	103
2	106
2.5	103
2.9	87
3.22–24	87
4.1, 18–20	100
14.19, 22	100
20.11	96
22	44

Exodus
1.17, 21	96
13.9, 16	37

Leviticus
17–26	97
19.14, 32	96
25.17	96

Deuteronomy
4.10	96
5.29	96
6.2	96
6.4–9	37
6.7	43
10.12f.	96
17.18–20	97
30.11–20	68, 93
32.6	100
32.18	101

Joshua
13.21	101

Judges
5.29	62
8.14	17
9.8	15
9.13	35
9.15	15
14.14	15
14.18	15

II Samuel
8.17	19
13.3	62
14.2	21
20.16	21
20.25	19
21.19	87
23.7	87

I Kings
3.4–15	89
3.5–15, 16–28	23
4.29–34	20, 23
7.2–7	91
10.1–13	20, 23
18.12	97

II Kings
6.6	87
14.9	15
17	96
17.7f.	96
17.25–28	97
17.35, 36, 38f.	96
18.18	19
22.8	19
25.11	102

II Chronicles
19.9	96

Ezra
7.6, 11, 12	28
7.14	29
7.25	28

Nehemiah
5.9, 15	96

Job
10.11	101
11.6ff.	79
12.13	79, 89
15.7f.	79
28	12, 43, 79, 88, 89
28.1–22	107
28.12–19	43
28.15–19	87, 88
28.18	88
28.23–27	102
28.28	96, 98
38.4	99
38.36f.	79

Psalms
1.1	42
2.6	101
24.2	99
32.1	42
34.12ff.	97
34.12	96
41.2	42
49.3	79
57.4	81
61.8	81
68.29	81
78.54	100
78.69	99
83.12	101
85.10–13	81
89.15	81
102.26	99
104.5, 24	99

Index of Biblical References

Psalms		Proverbs		Proverbs	
111.10	41, 96	1.29	73, 74, 75, 95, 98	3.1–10	41ff., 46, 64, 73
112.1	42				
119.1	42	1.30–33	74	3.1–4	33
119.105	49	1.32f.	76	3.1–3	76
128.1	42	1.33	74	3.1f.	64
136.5	99	2	31, 34	3.1	77
139.13	100, 101	2.1ff.	33, 34	3.2	35, 68, 76
		2.1–19	40f.	3.3	37, 41, 77
Proverbs		2.1–11	40	3.4	35, 63, 68, 76
1–7	30	2.1–6	98		
1.1ff.	33	2.1–4	40	3.5–12	30
1.1–5	37ff., 73, 75	2.1	34, 41, 73, 74, 76	3.5–10	42, 62
				3.5–8	66
1.1	20, 38, 52	2.2–8	35, 40, 41, 72	3.5f.	64
1.2–5	98			3.5	63
1.2, 3	62	2.2–4	73, 74, 79	3.6	65
1.4	76	2.2	35, 74, 76	3.7	62, 63
1.5	30, 65	2.3f.	74	3.8	42, 65
1.6	38	2.4	87	3.9f.	66
1.7	30, 38, 72, 73, 75, 95, 96, 98	2.5–8	29, 40, 73, 74, 75	3.9	63
				3.10	65, 68
		2.5	95, 98	3.11f.	42
1.8ff.	33	2.6	75, 98	3.11	33
1.8–19	39, 46, 73	2.9–11	40, 77	3.13–26	34
1.8f.	33, 34, 76	2.9	34, 40, 41, 62, 68, 73, 76	3.13–20	42, 72
1.8	36, 62, 65			3.13–18	42, 43, 46, 73, 74, 75, 79, 99
1.9	35, 41, 45, 77				
		2.10–15	41		
1.10–19	66	2.10f.	35, 72, 73, 74, 79	3.13–15	76, 87
1.10–15	67			3.14f.	87
1.10	33, 39	2.10	41, 77	3.15	88
1.11	39	2.12–22	40	3.16ff.	13
1.15–18	63	2.12–15	40, 41	3.16–18	76
1.15	33, 63	2.16–19	40, 73, 90	3.18	46, 87
1.16	39	2.16	47, 49, 67	3.19f.	30, 43, 73, 75, 98, 99, 104
1.18f.	62	2.17	63, 66		
1.19	44, 67	2.18f.	48, 49, 62		
1.20ff.	79, 80, 81	2.18	51	3.19	103
1.20–33	12, 71, 73, 74	2.19	41, 51, 62, 68	3.21ff.	33, 34
				3.21–31	43f.
1.20–28	74	2.20–22	40, 41	3.21–24	34, 73, 76
1.20f.	77	2.20	40, 41	3.21f.	77
1.20	79, 84, 85	2.21, 22	41	3.21	35, 36
1.22ff.	77	3–7	34	3.22	35, 41, 77
1.22	76, 77	3.1ff.	33	3.23f.	35, 43

114

Index of Biblical References

Proverbs		Proverbs		Proverbs	
3.23	36, 62	4.13	35, 46, 72, 73, 77, 79, 87	5.14, 15–20	48
3.24	48, 77			5.20	48, 49
3.25–35	43			5.21	48, 62, 63, 64, 73
3.25f.	43, 72	4.14–19	66		
3.26, 27–32	73	4.14–18	73	6.1–19	30, 33, 48
3.27–31	43	4.14f.	63	6.1, 20ff.	33
3.27–30	43	4.16–18	67	6.20–32	48f.
3.27f.	66, 67	4.18f.	62, 68	6.20–22	34, 73
3.29f.	66	4.18	46, 63	6.20	36, 49
3.30f.	67	4.19	46, 63	6.21	35, 37, 41, 77
3.31–35	44	4.20ff.	33, 34		
3.31	43, 44, 46	4.20–27	46f., 73	6.22	35, 68
3.32–35	43, 44	4.20–22	33	6.23	49, 72, 73
3.32	44, 62, 63, 64	4.20f.	36	6.24ff.	90
		4.20	46, 65	6.24f.	50, 67, 73
4.1ff.	33	4.21f.	77	6.24	40
4.1–9	44	4.21	35, 77	6.25, 26, 27, 28	49
4.1–5	44f.	4.22	35, 68, 76, 77	6.32	49, 62, 65, 67, 73
4.1–4	73				
4.1f.	34	4.23	66		
4.1	34, 62, 65	4.24–27	67	6.33–35	49
4.3–5	45	4.24	66	7.1ff.	33
4.4	44, 70	4.25–27	63, 66	7.1–27	49f.
4.5–9	35	4.25f.	63	7.1–3	34, 73
4.5	44, 45, 70, 72, 73, 74, 79, 87	4.26f.	47	7.2	35, 77
		4.26	63	7.3	35, 37, 41, 77
		5.1ff.	33		
4.6–9	45, 72, 73, 77, 79	5.1–11	40	7.4	35, 50, 72, 73, 74, 77, 79, 89
		5.1–8	41, 47		
4.6	44, 89	5.1–6	40, 73		
4.7f.	76	5.1f.	33	7.5ff.	90
4.7	44, 87	5.1	35, 62, 65, 94	7.5–27	13
4.8f.	80, 89			7.5	40, 47, 50, 67, 73
4.9	45, 77	5.3ff.	90		
4.10ff.	33, 34	5.3–8	48	7.6–23	50
4.10–19	45f.	5.3–6	62	7.6f.	50
4.10–12	34, 64, 68, 73, 76	5.3	67	7.7	76
		5.4–6	67	7.11f.	50
4.10f.	63, 76	5.5	48, 49, 63	7.16	106
4.10	35, 65, 68, 76	5.6	63, 67, 68	7.22f.	50
		5.7	33, 47, 50	7.24	33, 47, 50
4.11–15	46	5.8	48, 63, 73	7.25–27	73
4.11f.	36, 63	5.9–23	48	7.25	50, 63
4.11	35, 62	5.9–14	48	7.26f.	49
4.12	48, 68, 77	5.12–22	40	7.27	41, 50, 51

115

Index of Biblical References

Proverbs		Proverbs		Proverbs	
8f.	30, 72, 83f., 84	9.6	77	24.7	79
8	12, 80, 90, 103, 106	9.7–12	30, 72	24.21	20
		9.7	84f.	24.23	18
8.1ff	79, 81	9.10	85, 96, 98	25.1ff.	20
8.1–35	12	9.13–18	13, 73, 76, 78, 92, 104	25.1, 2–7	20
8.1–21	73, 74			25.6f.	71
8.1–3	77	9.18	41, 76, 85	29.4	20
8.1	34	10–29	20, 24ff., 27f., 30, 31, 71, 105	29.11	65
8.6–9	76			29.14	20
8.10	76, 87			30.1ff.	70
8.11	88	10.1ff.	20	30.14	40
8.13	73, 74, 75, 95, 98	10.17	49	31.1ff.	70
		10.27	96	31.1–9	52
		11.30	87	31.10	88
8.14	89	13.12	87		
8.15f.	12, 79, 89	13.15	41	*Song of Solomon*	
8.18	74, 76	13.24	67	3.11	89
8.19	87, 103	14.28	20	4.9–12	77, 89
8.20, 21	76	14.35	20, 71	5.1	77, 89
8.22–31	12, 29, 30, 32, 73, 74, 75, 79, 88, 90, 98, 99ff.	15.4	87	7.2	102
		15.33	96, 98		
		16.2	24	*Isaiah*	
		16.6	96	5.21	22, 23
		16.10–15	20	7.1–17	22
8.22–29	102	16.14f.	71	8.1	17
8.22	99, 100f.	16.16	87, 88	11.2f.	96
8.23–26	99, 103	16.30	40	11.2	23, 89
8.23	99, 101	17.27f.	65	25.7	101
8.24f.	99, 101	18.24	40	28.5	89
8.30f.	102f.	19.8	40	28.23–29	23
8.30	99, 101ff.	19.12	20	28.29	23
8.32–36	73, 74, 75	20.2	20, 71	29.13–15	22, 23
8.32	76	20.8, 26, 28	20	29.13f.	97
8.34	75, 76	21.1	20	30.1	101
8.35	73, 74, 75, 77, 87	21.23	65	30.14	40
		22.11	20	31.2	23, 83, 93
8.36	87	22.15	67	33.6	96
9.1ff.	79	22.17–23.11	16, 19, 24	36	17f.
9.1–6	12f., 73, 76, 77f., 79, 89, 92, 104	22.17	18	48.13	99
		22.22	24	59.7	39
		22.23	24, 65	61.10	89
		22.29	20	62.3	89
9.1	19, 79, 84, 85, 90ff.	23.1–3	71		
		23.13	67	*Jeremiah*	
9.3	84	23.14	24	4.14, 21	77

116

Index of Biblical References

Jeremiah	
4.22	22, 23
5.1	77
7.2	77
9.23f.	22
10.12	23
17.1	37
17.5–11	23
18.18	18, 22
31.33	37
39.9	102
44.17f.	105
50.10	84
52.15	101f.

Lamentations	
4.5	102

Ezekiel	
7.26	22
23	13, 81
25.10	84
28	20
32.30	101
37.16ff.	87

Hosea	
2.7	42
8.5	77

Amos	
8.10	44

Micah	
5.4	101

Wisdom	
7ff.	11

Ecclesiasticus	
1	11
1.14	98
24	11
24.6–12	95
38.24ff.	18
39.1–8	95
51.23	91

I Corinthians	
1.24	11

Colossians	
1.15–17	11
2.3	11

INDEX OF SUBJECTS

After-life, doctrine of, 24, 69
Ahaz, 22
Aḥiqar, Words of, 46, 51, 84, 86f.
Amarna Letters, 19
Amenemhēt, Instruction of, 35, 38, 53
Amen-em-opet, Instruction of, 16, 20, 25, 35, 36f., 38f., 51f., 53, 56, 57–61, 62, 64
Amennakht, Instruction of, 35, 36
Amesha Spentas, the, 80
'āmōn, 101–3
Anii, Wisdom of, 35, 51, 53, 59, 60, 70
Apophis, Myth of, 103
Aramaic literature, 84, 86f.
Astarte, see Ištar-Astarte
Aten, 57f.

Babylonia, Babylonians, 15, 16, 19, 35
Babylonian education, 15, 16
Babylonian wisdom, 15, 35, 38, 51, 82, 85
Ben Sira, 21
'Book of the Ten Discourses', the, 33–52, 53, 61–71, 72–76, 77, 78, 92, 93, 94, 95, 105f.
  additions to, 72ff.

Canaanites, the, 62, 83ff.
Cheti, Instruction of, 53
Christology, 11f.
Counsels of Wisdom, The, 51
Creation, views of, 11, 12, 43, 63, 64, 81f., 88, 90–92, 98–104, 106f.
Creation stories, 99, 103, 106f.
Cult and wisdom, 14, 26, 59, 66, 82f., 89

Descent of Ishtar into the Nether World, The, 51

Deutero-Isaiah, 106
Deuteronomy, Book of, 37, 51, 97

Ecclesiastes, Book of, 12, 15, 17, 27f., 61
Ecclesiasticus, Book of, 11, 12, 17, 21, 27, 28, 29, 30, 106
Education, Babylonian, 15, 16
Education, Egyptian, 16f., 19, 35f., 38, 45, 52, 53, 60, 61, 62, 67, 69–71, 105
Education, Israelite, 13f., 17f., 19, 21, 27, 31, 33ff., 62ff., 76, 91, 94, 95, 97f.
Egypt, Egyptians, 15ff., 31, 35ff., 45, 52, 53ff., 105, 106
Egyptian wisdom, 15–17, 19, 20f., 25, 26, 27, 35ff., 53–61, 62f., 64, 65, 66, 67, 68, 69–71, 78, 82f., 93
El, 62, 83, 85f., 100f.
Elders, 22
Enuma Eliš, 103
'ēṣā, 18
Exodus, Book of, 21
Ezra, 28f., 30, 31

Fear of Yahweh, the, 95–98
Folly, as woman, 13, 29, 104
formulae, introductory, 33ff.

Genesis, Book of, 21
Gnosticism, 12, 104
God and the gods, concepts of, 24, 26, 35, 52, 55, 56–59, 62, 63–65, 68, 69, 75, 81f., 83–87, 89f., 92–104, 105–7
Greek Fathers, the, 12
Greek thought, influence of, 19, 106

118

Index of Subjects

ḥākām, 18, 62
Herodotus, 90
Hezekiah, 20
Hike, 82
ḥokmā, 11, 46, 61f., 79
ḥokmōt, 11, 79, 84, 85
ḥōlaltī, 101
Holiness Code, the, 97
Hu, 81
Hypostases, divine, in the ancient near east, 13, 81f.

Ideal man, the, 59–61, 65–67
Individual, importance of in wisdom literature, 14f., 17, 22, 26, 37, 51, 61, 68
Instructions, Egyptian, 16, 35ff., 53–61
Iranian thought, influence of, 80, 91
Isaiah, 17, 21–23
Isaiah, Book of, 37
Isis-Osiris myth, the, 88
Isis-Sophia speculation, 80
Ištar, see Ištar-Astarte
Ištar-Astarte, 80, 88, 89f., 91, 92

Jeremiah, 21f.
Jeremiah, Book of, 37
Job, Book of, 12, 14, 15, 17, 27f., 61
John, Gospel of, 11
Joseph, 21

Kemit, the, 45
Khnūm, 57, 58
Kings, First Book of, 20, 21, 23

Law, the, 11, 21, 28f.
Logos, the, 11

maat, 54–56, 61, 62, 78
Mandaean literature, 90
Merikerē, Instruction for, 38, 51, 53, 56, 58, 59, 60, 64, 70

Mesopotamia, Mesopotamian wisdom, see Babylonia, Babylonian wisdom
mūsār, 46, 62, 67

Nehemiah, 28, 30
Nissaktī, 101, 102

'Onchsheshonqy, Instruction of, 53, 56
Order, concept of, 61–63
Osiris, 24, 88

Papyrus Insinger, 25, 53
personifications in O.T., 12
Phoenician literature, 84, 85
Priests, Israelite, 18, 25
Prophets, attitude to wisdom of the, 18, 21–24, 25, 26, 51, 77
Proverbs, Book of, literary problems of, 13f., 19f., 26f., 29–32
religion of, 24–27
Proverbs, popular, 21
Ptahhotep, Instruction of, 35, 36, 39, 51, 53, 54, 55f., 56, 58, 59, 60, 70

qānānī, 75, 100f., 101, 102

Rē, 57
Rē-Atum, 81
Religion, Egyptian, 24f., 54–59, 61–65, 69, 81f.
Retribution, concepts of, 17, 42, 44, 55, 57f., 61, 62, 63, 64, 65, 68, 93

Scribal schools, 19, 21
Scribes, 16ff., 21, 28f., 52
seboyet, 62, 67, 78
Sehetepibrē, Instruction of, 35
Seraiah, 19
Sexual cult, theory of, 89f., 92
Shachar and Shalim, 100
Shaphan, 19
Shay and Renenut, 57

Index of Subjects

Sheba, Queen of, 20
Shebna, 19
Sheva, 19
Sia, 81
'silent man', the, 59–61, 65
Solomon, 20f., 21, 23, 52
sōpēr, sōperīm, 17f., 28
Spirit of God, the, 11
'strange woman', the, 13, 29, 40f., 47–50, 90, 91
Šuruppak, Instructions of, 35, 38

Thoth, 57
Tyre, wisdom of, 20

Ugaritic texts, 62, 84ff.
Urmensch, 88

Wisdom as bride, 77, 79, 87, 89f.
  as Canaanite goddess, 83–87
  as conferring gifts on men, 11, 24, 75, 76ff.
  as divine attribute, 23, 78ff., 98ff.
  as hostess, 12f., 77, 79
  as human attribute, 12, 15, 22, 23, 35, 75, 94
  as hypostasis, 11, 13, 21
  as poetical figure, 13, 80–82
  as preacher, 77, 79
  as precious object, 12, 79, 87–89
  as teacher, 13, 74, 77, 91
  as theological principle, 11, 106f.
  as woman, 12f., 13, 77, 79, 81, 82ff., 89ff.
  Babylonian, 15, 35, 38, 51, 82, 85
  Canaanite, 19f., 83–85
  didactic, 15f., 27f.
  Egyptian, 15–17, 19, 20f., 25, 26, 27, 35ff., 53–61, 62f., 64, 65, 66, 67, 68, 69–71, 78, 28f., 93
  house of, 12f., 19, 77, 79, 90–92
  in later Judaism, 11, 20, 21, 28f., 49, 107
  incarnate in Christ, 11f.
  Israelite, development of, 14–29, 72ff.
  Israelite, foreign influences on, 15ff., 69–71, 80ff.
  mythological influence on, 13, 78, 82–92, 103f.
  personification of, 11ff., 21, 28, 29, 31, 80ff.
  practical, 15
  pre-existence of, 11, 12, 87f., 90f., 98ff.
  reflective, 15f., 27f.
  role of at the Creation, 11, 12, 88, 90–92, 98–104, 106f.
  royal, 20f., 23, 38, 89
  seven pillars of, the, 90–92
'wisdom literature', meaning of, 14, 17
Wisdom of Solomon, The, 11, 12, 104
Wisdom schools, 17, 19, 21ff., 52, 96, 97f.
Wisdom teachers, 16f., 19, 31, 33ff., 53, 62f., 64, 74, 97, 98
  authority of, 22, 35, 37, 45, 53, 58, 61, 64, 67–69, 70, 75, 76, 93, 94
Wisdom teaching, anthropocentricity of, 22, 26, 31, 68
Wise men, 18, 21, 22
Wise women, 21
Word of God, the, 11

www.ingramcontent.com/pod-product-compliance
Lightning Source LLC
Chambersburg PA
CBHW070929160426
43193CB00011B/1620